THE INNER ART
OF KARATE

BOOKS BY KENJI TOKITSU

The Complete Book of Five Rings
Ki and the Way of the Martial Arts
Miyamoto Musashi: His Life and Writings

THE INNER ART OF KARATE

Cultivating the Budo Spirit
in Your Practice

KENJI TOKITSU

*Translated by
Sherab Chödzin Kohn*

SHAMBHALA
Boston & London
2012

Shambhala Publications, Inc.
Horticultural Hall
300 Massachusetts Avenue
Boston, Massachusetts 02115
www.shambhala.com

9 8 7 6 5 4 3 2 1

First Edition

Printed in the United States of America

⊛ This edition is printed on acid-free paper that meets the American National Standards Institute z39.48 Standard.
♻ This book is printed on 30% postconsumer recycled paper. For more information please visit us at www.shambhala.com.

Distributed in the United States by Random House, Inc., and in Canada by Random House of Canada Ltd

Designed by James D. Skatges

Library of Congress Cataloging-in-Publication Data
Tokitsu, Kenji, 1947–
The inner art of karate: cultivating the budo spirit
in your practice / Kenji Tokitsu; translated by
Sherab Chödzin Kohn.
p. cm.
Includes bibliographical references.
ISBN 978-1-59030-949-0 (pbk.: alk. paper)
1. Karate. I. Title.
GV1114.3.T638 2012
796.815'3—dc23
2011027565

CONTENTS

THE INNER ART
OF KARATE

INTRODUCTION

ONE DAY, on my way to high school in the springtime light, as I was walking along a raised dirt road through the rice paddies in the company of the black blotch of my shadow, I made an attempt to really walk, to be present in each step—but it didn't work. The sensation of not-being that I felt then and my failed attempt to be in a real way are what got me started on my quest for the existence of the self in the martial arts. This experience reconnected me with a tradition of my culture that I had been drawn away from by my education—the typical education of Japanese youth in the aftermath of the Second World War. So I started practicing karate, not as a mere physical exercise, but in a deeper way—as a means of confirming my existence.

I had been very attracted by what I had heard in my childhood about the spiritual state attained by adepts of the way of the sword. Here was the ideal image of a human being as seen by Japanese culture. According to this conception, a person can attain self-perfection through deep and thorough study of a traditional art. In *budo* (which applies to all of the Japanese martial arts taken together), this state, this mode of existence in relating to oneself and others, can be attained through mastering techniques developed in the context of combat to the death.

Why did I pick karate rather than any of the other martial arts? I felt, considering the real presence of violence within our society, that the other martial arts practices (the sword, archery, etc.) had something anachronistic about them. Karate seemed to be more relevant to our times. Nevertheless, I do not view karate as a form of violence meant to serve my own purposes. Nor should we try to gauge the effectiveness of karate in comparison to firearms or in the framework of mass conflicts. As soon as we look at it that way, karate loses its meaning.

What I see in karate is a body of cultural knowledge that can lead a man or woman to a certain state of being. As Japanese feudal society saw it, the way of the martial arts was authoritative for the whole of existence. Even today I think we can see in it a means of enriching our lives and bringing balance to them. But in today's society, the way of the martial arts can no longer be regarded as an exclusive guideline for life. Such an approach is part of the worldview of a bygone era. Nowadays such a view can only lead to a kind of nostalgia-laden mysticism.

Nonetheless, for me, karate remains connected to the possibility of understanding the totality of my existence. I come back in this regard to the question I had as a teenager: can every moment in itself be lived deeply? I know now, from my own experience, that the practice of budo makes it possible, through the movement of the body, to more fully integrate the self into every moment. And this is the process I propose to explain in this book.

In our everyday life, for the most part, the consciousness of self engages only in a very loose way with just a few of our physical movements, or else it is absent altogether. This is the sign of a lagging-behind, a loss of synchronization, in relation to our body. This sense of being out of sync with the body is something that has been vividly felt in Western societies and is currently provoking a variety of critical reflections. In Japan, Western influence contrasts with the view of the traditional culture, according to which the aim of man is to enter into harmony with all that surrounds him. The idea is that what we call "the self" only exists as a result of a more universal unity, or nonduality, which encompasses both self and other; this "self" includes the body, our movements, and so on.

The learning process in budo begins with physical technique, but this is only a small part of it. What's more essential is that our subjectivity must be present in every moment and in all of our movements, and must also be present at the same time that we are relating with an adversary.

In the combat of budo, the presence of self in every movement becomes vital. Any loss of synchronization between our subjective mind and our movements constitutes a lapse, a fault, a moment of vulnerability. Our opponent will attack the moment he detects such a fault, and thus he will provide us with an instant critique on a very concrete level. In ordinary life, where such ripostes do not occur, we are spared having to be aware of our every movement. In combat, in order to ward off attack, our awareness must first relate to our own movements before engaging with those of the adversary.

For this reason, I see karate as a way of exploring and putting to the test our relationship with our own movements, and beyond that with our body as a whole. And it is only after the density of self has been heightened through the practice of budo that combat at a high level becomes approachable. On that level, it is necessary to perceive the other and maintain awareness of self at the same time. In this book, I want to shed light on the specific nature of this relationship between self and other in the combat of budo.

It is possible for an elderly budo master, by which I mean someone over sixty years old, to defeat young men who are only twenty or thirty years old, even though they are well trained and endowed with considerable physical strength. The reason is that physical strength and physical technique are not the primary factors in the combat of budo—which is not the case in other combat sports.

Adepts of budo who practiced their art throughout their lives and reached a level where they could be called masters were fairly common in feudal Japanese society.[1] Nowadays, we find only a very few such adepts in martial arts such as kendo, aikido, judo, karate-do, and so on.

The traditional Japanese martial arts have been introduced into various foreign countries under the name of budo, but in a form that does not correspond to the strict meaning of this word. They have begun to develop within the framework of combat sports and are understood by most of the people who practice them as sports, or as a kind of sport—perhaps a new "Oriental" sport.

But if we wish to understand what budo is in the strict sense of the term within the martial arts we practice, and if we then wish to practice these arts in the way that will bring us the most benefit, we must stop looking at them as sports, because in that framework we can only have a superficial and distorted view of them. Instead, we must gain an understanding of the full scope of the cultural phenomenon of budo. We must study in depth this physical expression that is linked with a certain state of mind as it was formed by traditional Japanese culture. To reduce budo to a mere physical activity is to throw away the flesh of the orange and just keep the peel.

So if the word *budo* can be translated as "martial arts," it is only to the extent that we stop considering the martial arts as belonging to the realm of sport. Understood in a strict sense, budo has many dimensions, whereas combat sports generally have only one: physical strength associated with techniques of physical movement. This dimension, along with the apparent aim of winning, is one that budo and combat sports share. This is why there is such a strong tendency to conflate them. But identifying budo as a combat sport would lead us to content ourselves with understanding it through the logic of sports, where the role of the body is conceived in a dualistic way—in terms of the separation of body and mind. This dualistic conception, however, is of no help to us when it comes to understanding the profound nature of budo.

The examination of budo requires a different approach, one whose roots reach down beyond the level of physical expression.

We will not be able to practice budo in the real sense until we have grasped it in its totality. Again, how can we explain by means of a theory of sports that an elderly master can defeat in combat, flawlessly and with ease, a well-trained young opponent who clearly has the advantage in terms of muscular strength and physical endurance?

Two kinds of explanation of this phenomenon tend to arise as long as we fail to adopt a multidimensional perspective. First, there is the one in which we deny the facts by telling ourselves, "This is a trick" or "This is just a movie," and conclude that there was no real combat involved. Alternatively, we might accept the phenomenon by saying, "There is something besides physical strength in play here; the master possesses some force beyond my knowledge, some force that cannot be explained." In this second approach, we accept into our reasoning the idea of some mystical force, such as the myth of a mental force or a shout that can kill. (We must not confuse the genuine elderly budo master with aged Orientals disguised as masters who embellish their role by making ambiguous, mystical pronouncements. Right from the beginning, we must free ourselves from the kinds of images and ideas that are associated with these phony masters, who tend to play to the psychological needs of Westerners. Often in these cases, the "master" is acting as a front for some sort of commercial activity.)

In this book, I am going to try to analyze the multidimensional structure of budo, particularly the bare-handed budo disciplines, using karate as the example. This should help make it possible to achieve in karate, understood as budo, an extremely high level of development of a form of physical practice that is rooted in the totality of the person. It should help us to find a method, more theoretical than empirical, for attaining the very highest level of budo, which a few warriors (samurai) of the Japanese feudal period, and a very few among the budo practitioners of the present era, have been able to attain—without themselves being able to show how they were able to do it.

This, of course, raises the question whether it is even possible to revive in contemporary form a cultural achievement that dates back several centuries. But I believe it can be done. By studying the writings of our predecessors, particularly the sword masters of the feudal period, it is possible to find a starting point for reestablishing budo in contemporary life, patently different though the social context may be. In doing this, I will bring a study of the works of the principal budo masters of former times together with my own experience of the practice.

Theoretical research based on written documents by earlier practitioners of budo must inevitably face a number of difficulties. First of all, we must situate these writings in terms of the particular qualities of the culture in which they appeared. The most important texts on budo were written by men of the sword of the seventeenth and eighteenth centuries, a period in which theoretical thought, systematic logic, and science were not at all highly developed in Japan. These writings are not at all organized in such a way as to accommodate an objective, explanatory analysis, nor do they facilitate explications of the meaning of the terms employed. Their authors wrote in an intuitive and empirical way, often making use of comparisons from the natural world.

Thus, regarding states of mind occurring during sword combat, Yagyu Munenori writes that in the moment before the onset of combat, it is necessary to have a mental state whose surface is calm but whose depths are in motion.[2] This is what is called "hearing the sound of wind-water." Wind by itself does not make any sound. It produces a noise when it touches an object. That is why, when it is moving in the heights, it is calm, but when it is moving lower down, it makes noise by touching objects, such as bamboo, trees, and so on. In such a mental state as this, when you are not moving on the outside (your body), it is necessary for the inside (your awareness) to be in motion. This can be likened to a bird on the water: though on the outside it is seen to be floating calmly, its feet are in continuous motion.

On the subject of distance in combat, the same author writes,

You must assess the distance at which your opponent's sword cannot touch you. You approach the opponent without his noticing—this is like the reflection of the moon appearing in water. You must have in your mind a moon place and a water place before beginning the combat.

The reader is supposed to grasp intuitively the meaning of these phrases and words in relation to his own experience and practice. A complete understanding is not reached until the subjective mind of the author and the subjective mind of the reader coincide. Moreover, these writings are very often based on the values and worldview of the warriors of this period (an amalgam of Shinto, Buddhism, Confucianism, the ideal of the warrior, and so on), which they in turn reinforce.

The remarks of authors on budo as a practical technique of combat often make reference to their ideas on religion, morals, and ethics. Following are some examples:

The sword is the starting point for the tactics of the sword, because it is on the basis of the virtue of the sword that one rules the world and oneself.

Ito Ittosai (seventeenth century) says that when in studying the way of the sword, "someone attains the supreme level, he has no need to think or to trouble his mind, nor to attach too much importance to the mind, because the movement of his mind and his body are in perfect fusion, and from that point on, there is no difference between evil and good."

Matsuura Seizan (eighteenth century) writes,

When you strike downward from above with the sword, it is desirable not to see your opponent's sword and to have a completely empty state of mind. You must strike relying entirely on a god, whichever one it may be, driving away the thought

of self; and you must not think that you are striking with
your own force.

Gichin Funakoshi (twentieth century), in a text entitled *Twenty
Precepts on the Way of Karate*, writes, "Karate-do is an extension of
morality." (The word we translate here as "morality" has a broader
sense in Japanese and could as well be translated by "right mind.")

I believe it is important, in investigating these writings, to eliminate the parts that have no essential connection with the practice
of budo. By doing this, we can better reestablish budo as a practical
science in the social life of the present time. We must not only
study these accounts in a theoretical and analytical manner, but
also rely on experience of the practice of budo. I regard this as the
best, if not the only, way to grasp the meaning of the intuitive and
analogical expressions found in these classical documents.

Until now, no study has been made of these writings from this
point of view. One reason is the difficulty of interpreting these
documents. However, another reason relates to a more general social phenomenon.

Since the end of the nineteenth century, modernization has
been a dominant trend in Japanese society. This has been accomplished by importing cultural elements and scientific techniques—
both of them equally sophisticated—from Western countries.
And as the economy of Japan has grown more capitalistic, many of
these imported elements and techniques have been further improved upon. In the course of this social evolution, many of the
ancient practices and cultural achievements of Japan have been either destroyed or, when preserved, regarded only as mementos of
the past—but they have never been treated as being truly compatible with Japan's modernization.[3] Since much of our cultural heritage has still not found its place in the life of our modern society,
it is set apart and remains on the margins of contemporary culture.
Budo is no exception to this.

Here we come back to a question we raised earlier. Is it possible
to prolong the life of budo in the present situation without de-

stroying its essence? The same question applies to the other traditional Japanese arts. In the course of the modernization and Westernization of Japan, the practice of budo has continued to be regarded as an antimodern phenomenon. In fact many of those practicing budo have understood their activity not in the sense of re-creating budo's place in human life, but rather as a reaction against the ongoing social changes. That is why, as the development of capitalist society in Japan has progressed, the gap between the country's real social life and the practice of budo has continued to grow—to the point where budo now seems to be an anachronism. Moreover, contemporary practitioners of budo have not succeeded in going beyond the intuitive, empirical, religious, and ethical conceptions of budo created by the samurai within the feudal context.

For contemporary budo practitioners, there is a contradiction between their way of life in capitalist Japanese society (in which they participate socially in the production and consumption of goods) and the practice and teaching of budo. The reason for this is that the concepts connected with budo remain those inherited from the warriors of the past, who looked down upon the activities and values connected with producing and consuming goods. The greater the value placed on their art by contemporary practitioners of budo, the deeper the contradiction they encounter between the practice of budo and their social life, which is based on a system of commodities.

In short, in this situation, they have, on the one hand, either faithfully reproduced their budo art as a mode of traditional practice or, on the other, assimilated it to the idea of sport imported from Western countries and thus reduced it to a single dimension. The first attitude has tended to promote mystification, whereas the second has resulted in a deterioration of quality associated with a misunderstanding of the real content of budo. At the same time, these mistaken attitudes have contributed to an increase in the number of people practicing it.

Breaking with both of these attitudes, my intention here is to examine budo within the new social context, with a view to recon-stituting it as a practice that can be fully integrated with contem-porary life. That is why this book aims to provide an analysis and theory of budo that can lead to true progress on the path of budo seen in all its multiple dimensions. Establishing budo on a renewed theoretical foundation should make it possible for us to go beyond an extremely poverty-stricken repetition of the heritage of earlier times.

To accomplish this task, I intend to employ a dialectical method, linking my own practice of budo with a newly elaborated theoreti-cal foundation.

1

WHAT IS KARATE?

KARATE SHOULD NOT be viewed as a mere technique of combat, nor should it be seen as a sport, and still less as a kind of show. It is, rather, a continuation of budo, the Japanese tradition of the martial arts.

Budo, as an art of the feudal warriors of Japan, was a way of life centered around the practice of techniques of combat and oriented toward attainment of a certain level of perfection. Without doubt, since those times the conditions of life have changed, but it remains true that karate has no meaning except in connection with the development of the person of the practitioner in his or her totality.

The literal translation of the Japanese word *karate* is "bare hand." Its general context is that of budo. It is a technique of combat with the bare hands in which one remains at a distance from the opponent. This is the reason for the importance in karate of punches and kicks to vital points of the opponent's body and, when the opponent is closer, of holds and throws. The approach toward technique in karate is based on the notion that the opponent can be defeated with a single blow. For this reason, the vital points (as determined by the discipline of acupuncture) are utilized. And for the same reason, the *karateka* must cultivate precision and the concentration of force in the delivery of blows.

Karate was developed for bare-handed combat with adversaries who could be expected to be armed with bladed weapons. For the karateka, in addition to his bare hands, any object that could be picked up and held in the hands could also become a weapon—for example, the *nunchaku* (two sticks joined together, originally a farmer's flail), the *tonfa* (a stick), and the *bo* (a short piece of wood with a perpendicularly mounted handle, also derived from a farming tool). These do not require distinct techniques but only an extension of the movements of karate.

In Japanese, the word *kara-te* consists of *kara* (empty) and *te* or *de* (hand). This written form and its meaning were introduced around 1936 by Gichin Funakoshi to describe the martial art he was teaching. He modified an old term, *to-de* (Chinese hand).

THE ORIGINS

In Okinawa, bare-handed combat became highly developed during periods of oppression when the bearing of arms was forbidden to the local population. During the fifteenth century, the island was subjected to Chinese rule. At that time, in order to prevent uprisings, all weapons were prohibited. Thus the inhabitants began using and developing ancient techniques of bare-handed combat, enriching them with elements borrowed from the various Chinese "arts of the fist."

Then at the beginning of the seventeenth century, Okinawa was conquered by a Japanese feudal lord, who maintained the ban on bearing arms.[1] In order to be able to defend themselves against their armed occupiers, the inhabitants of Okinawa continued to work intensively on bare-handed combat. Training was done clandestinely, in small groups; this led to the differentiation of various styles, even in the interior of the island. These were called *shurit-te*, *naha-te*, and *tomorino-te* after their region of origin. These techniques of combat taken all together were known as *okinawa-te*, or to-de. The differences between the regional styles resulted partly from the transmission of techniques from different regions of China and partly from particular local characteristics in Okinawa.

In the course of the nineteenth century, Okinawa was assimilated into Japanese culture, and the significance of the bare-handed fighting techniques changed. In the first decade of the twentieth century, the educational value of okinawa-te was recognized, and the decision was taken to teach it in the Okinawan schools. Anko Itosu and Kanryo Higaonna were appointed to supervise this educational endeavor, and they achieved a certain level of formalization of okinawa-te. This was the situation in which the adepts were trained who would transmit their art beyond Okinawan shores.

The first demonstrations by Gichin Funakoshi in Japan (1916 in Kyoto, 1922 in Tokyo) were highly successful and aroused the curiosity of practitioners of the traditional Japanese martial arts with whom Funakoshi came in contact. The success of okinawa-te received official recognition when Funakoshi was appointed to teach his discipline at several universities. To begin with, he had only a few students, but they were very enthusiastic.

Some years after Funakoshi, a number of other masters of karate (still known at the time as okinawa-te or to-de), such as Kenwa Mabuni and Chojun Miyagi, developed different styles in the regions where they established themselves. All of these men were considered at that time to be masters of a very high level.

I am taking Funakoshi as a primary example because his arrival provides a means of dating the beginnings of karate in Japan and also because it was he who introduced the term *karate*. It so happens that the author of the present book is a practitioner of the style of karate he introduced (*shotokan*). However, this should not be taken to mean that Funakoshi's style was superior.

The art of bare-handed combat existed in Japan under the name *jujutsu*. This was one of the eighteen disciplines that warriors of the classical period were supposed to practice. With the advent of the modern era (1868), the bearing of arms was outlawed in Japan and the martial arts went into decline. However, jujutsu, transformed into a sport and now called "judo," went through a period of major development. This was the situation when karate appeared in Japan.

Funakoshi was very much attracted to traditional Japanese culture, which he studied intensively. He imbued the notion of budo with further significance, particularly through his connection with Jigoro Kano, the founder of judo, and Hakudo Nakayama, a master of the sword.

At this point, the way the term *karate* was formed is of considerable interest, because it reflects Funakoshi's effort to achieve a fusion of his art with budo. At first the term represented only a change of name. *To-de* became *kara-te* (retaining the sense of "Chinese hand"), and then the term *jutsu* (technique) was added, yielding the term *karate-jutsu*. But since *te* (hand) also means "technique" in Japanese, Funakoshi did away with this added element and changed the meaning of the term *kara*. *Kara-te* was now taken to mean "empty hand." Finally, still later, Funakoshi added the notion of *do* (way or path), giving us *karate-do*. (For more on the definition of *do*, see chapter 2.) This final step reflects his desire to see his art become integrated with budo through a qualitative transformation of its practice. His term, *karate-do*, was finally accepted by the other masters of his period.

The choice of the meaning "empty" for the word *kara* was not unrelated to the influence of Zen Buddhism on the martial arts. The word *kara* has a double meaning: the most obvious one is "empty" as in "empty hand," but there is an implicit reference here to a broader meaning of "empty," which has to do with the state of mind necessary for the practice of karate. Funakoshi's choice of meaning here without a doubt reflected his desire for a deepening of his art that would enable it to be integrated with budo. In the course of its development, budo was strongly influenced by Zen Buddhism, which helped define its mental aspect as well as its outer form and even the way in which its techniques were practiced. "Emptiness," understood as a state of mind to be sought after, is where Zen and budo come together.

Responding to the emperor On, who asked him what the fundamental principle of the holy doctrine of the Buddha was, the monk Bodhidharma replied, "Unfathomable emptiness and nothing sacred."

Emptiness, as seen by Zen Buddhism, must be distinguished from mere nothingness. Those who taste emptiness do not let themselves be carried away into false conceptions of nothingness. We should not imagine emptiness as being nothing. Emptiness is the state of the mind in which, it could be said, the mind takes on a cosmic dimension.

> The man who holds to the mode of action of the Principle walks in simplicity and refrains from concerning himself with the many things.
>
> Holding to the origin, to the source, at one with the unity, he knows the way spirits do—by intuition within the Principle. As a result, his ability extends to everything.
>
> As soon as he meets a being, he perceives him, he penetrates him, he knows him through and through.
>
> —CHUANG TZU

It is extremely difficult to attain this state, which presupposes a new understanding of reality.

> When the mind is detached, emptiness appears.
> Emptiness is simply non-attachment.
> To understand emptiness of distinctions is to be liberated.[2]

In emptiness is also where we find the roots of to-de. We know that Bodhidharma (Daruma in Japanese) exercised considerable influence on the Chinese forms of bare-handed combat. Bodhidharma was an Indian Buddhist monk who came to China around 520 C.E. in order to spread the Buddhist teaching there. At first he led a wandering life, but eventually took up residence at Shaolin-su Monastery (Shorin-ji in Japanese).

His teaching was the point of departure for Zen Buddhism in China. It is related that to disciples who came to receive his teachings, he gave a method called Ekkinkyo, saying,

> The doctrine is taught for the mind, but mind and body are originally one and they cannot be separated.
>
> As I look at you right now, it appears that your mind, just like your body, is weak and tired, and you are incapable of attaining the goal you are seeking. That is why I am giving you a method in which I admonish you to increase the capacity of your body. After that, try to attain the essence of the doctrine.

This method was made up of physical training in which various movements were practiced in connection with work on the breath. The goal of the training was twofold: achieving good physical condition and achieving unity of mind and body. This method came out of the older lineage of Indian yoga, in which physical exercise is linked with pursuit of a spiritual state.

As to the physical techniques themselves, they were not new, and we can find traces in them of Indian and Chinese methods of combat. But Bodhidharma created a fresh synthesis of these physical techniques by applying them to an objective that was new in the history of the martial arts—the quest for a particular spiritual state.

Ekkinkyo became very widespread in China during Bodhidharma's lifetime. Sometime after his death, during a period of troubles in China, his monastery was destroyed, and the monks scattered to the four corners of China, where they propagated his method. It was probably during this period, in which traveling was dangerous, that the quality in Ekkinkyo of an art of combat came to the fore. It is generally thought that Ekkinkyo and Chinese boxing were the basis of *shaolin-su kempo*, a method of combat that spread throughout China at this time, and in all probability reached Okinawa. Shaolin-su kempo was developed in a variety of forms and continues to be practiced today. In its present form, it incorporates punches and kicks, throws and holds, as well as movements using a stick. It relies on a knowledge of sensitive points corresponding to those in acupuncture and Chinese massage.

This example of religion and the martial arts coming together is not the only one in the history of China. Taoism, which was for the most part the religion of the lower, oppressed social strata and of groups of rebels, was adopted as the basis for physical training in one variant of shaolin-su kempo, known as *buto ha kempo*, which was very intensively practiced by certain monks. This discipline was passed down through many periods when it was prohibited and had to be practiced clandestinely. In shaolin-su kempo, the technical aspect played a dominant role, while the main emphasis Bodhidharma had imparted fell away. For Bodhidharma—since mind and body are inseparable—a martial art could be a path toward the attainment of spiritual perfection. For him, the goal was to attain the ultimate truth through spiritual awakening (satori in Japanese). This could be achieved by relating directly to one's own experience and thus rediscovering the path followed by the Buddha—much in the same way that a Christian might follow in the footsteps of Jesus. Such a state of awakening cannot be attained unless there is a union of body and mind, which presupposes the purification of both. The practice of the martial arts was the means he proposed to his disciples for reaching this state.

For the warriors of the martial arts of Japan, a conception analogous to this was developed as a path to perfection. This reached its zenith during the Tokugawa (Edo) period (1603–1868).

Funakoshi's inspiration was to introduce this conception into okinawa-te, thus transforming it into karate-do. At the beginning this caused him to become the target of extremely violent criticism from certain masters of okinawa-te. Nevertheless, this was the view that came to characterize his school, the Shotokan.

Karate, practiced as okinawa-te, was a method of combat developed purely with the aim of achieving immediate effectiveness. But its integration into Japanese budo gave it a much more profound dimension and transformed the way it was practiced. Effectiveness (defeating the adversary) remains a goal, but it is not the only one. The karateka's training and his journey toward perfection of body and mind retain primary importance for him even if he never has the opportunity to experience real combat. As Funakoshi wrote in his *Twenty Principles of Karate-do*, karate is the manifestation of right mind.

This approach to karate was not without its problems. Funakoshi and other men of the martial arts of his period did not sufficiently consider the fact that the social context had changed since the time of the Japanese warriors. The difficulties that arose from this were particularly acute for karate, which was just then trying to become a form of budo. It had to deal with the rigidity of the *budokas*, who viewed budo as a permanent value and failed to see that certain aspects of it were connected with a particular historical period.

Karate contains technical elements that are very ancient, in which the Chinese tradition and the local Okinawan tradition are blended, fused together into a method of combat that responded to the conditions of the lives of the inhabitants of Okinawa. All through the history of what eventually became karate, a traditional teaching was transmitted that was then readjusted to fit the experience and personality of its masters.

The technical knowledge of karate is codified into katas, which are specific sequences of movements that are repeated in the course of training and that serve as a support for the transmission of this knowledge. (We will look more deeply into the notion of kata in chapter 4.)

The names of the katas are a living reflection of certain aspects of the history of karate. They may express either the significance of the kata, one aspect of it, its origin, or the manner in which it was transmitted.[3] (By "significance of the kata," I mean the particular techniques that it employs or the goal it seeks to achieve.) The following katas may be taken as examples:

Nijiushiho: "twenty-four steps."

Gojiushiho: "fifty-four steps." Each step contains a technique—this is the most obvious level. At a deeper level, each technique contains several techniques.

Sochin: "violence" or "force" (*so*) and "calm" (*chin*). Certain passages in this kata simultaneously require violence, or force, and calm.

Heian (*pinan* in Chinese): "state of peace and calm." There are five katas with this name, all of which are fundamental to the learning process. Contrary to what is generally thought, these are not beginners' katas, but rather have a profound significance that can only be discovered after long practice. The name of the kata is without doubt related to this more profound level. Moreover, Funakoshi said that if one wishes to learn the techniques of self-defense, it is more than sufficient to limit oneself to an in-depth study of these five katas.

Meikyo: literally, "clear mirror." A pure state of mind that reflects whatever is in front of it. The name of the kata evokes the condition of awareness sought after in carrying out the kata.

Kururunfa: "stop the oncoming attack and break through."

Bassai: "break " or "cut through" (*bas*) and "fortress" (*sai*). There are several katas with this name. One variant was transmitted by Master Matsumura and is known by the name *Matsumura-no-bassai*. It is possible to point to several katas named, in a similar fashion, after the person who transmitted them.

Empi: "flight of the swallows." This refers to the lightness and quickness that are necessary to execute this kata. Here the name does not express the significance of the kata, but rather a superficial aspect of it.

Gankaku: "the crane on the rock." Certain positions in this kata evoke this image.

Ji'in: "temple of the love of Buddha." The technique has no relation to this name. I think the name is a reference to the way in which the kata was transmitted—doubtless by temple monks.

Jion: "love of Buddha and gratitude." This is also a kata that was transmitted by the monks. The spiritual state that was most certainly connected with this kata at the beginning is no longer apparent in its movements.

Tekki: "iron horseman." There is doubtless a connection here with the to-de of the north of China, in which positions similar to the ones in this kata are practiced and where katas are practiced on horseback. Thus in the tekki kata, the position of the legs known as "horseman's posture" is of major importance.

Hangetsu: "half moon." The characteristic of this kata is that several times one places the feet, then moves them by tensing them in a certain way, so as to make them describe a semicircular movement similar to the shape of a half-moon.

THE COMPONENTS OF KARATE

Karate is a technique of combat with the bare hands in which the greatest possible effectiveness is sought but in which this cannot be achieved through physical means alone. In seeking maximal effectiveness, one inevitably enters into the realm of mind. This happens from the very moment one is engaged in combat with other people rather than merely breaking bricks or other objects.

It is often said that the goal of karate is to conquer oneself, but for me that is not the goal of karate. This description is in some ways a come-on, but in any case, it is an inadequate one. If one must conquer oneself, it is because there is a realm that cannot be reached except by doing so.

To take the simplest example, in the course of learning how to deliver a punch or a kick, it is necessary to go beyond the limits one has been attributing to oneself so as to reach *kime* (see chapter 2). This involves conquering oneself, one could say, for the sake of becoming more effective.

To go beyond one's limits in any aspect of combat, a physical and mental effort is necessary that opens up new possibilities for progress. An example of this would be that the goal of working with maintaining tension is not a permanent state of tension but rather a state of relaxation.

If the goal were just to conquer oneself, it would be better simply to practice Zen meditation! The study and practice of karate cannot be reduced to a religious quest, because karate is about fighting. It entails the question of life and death. In Zen, this problem is transcended because life and death are not regarded as separate; rather there is a continuity from one to the other, and the death of the body does not count as real death. In karate, on the other hand, the point of departure is concrete physical movements, and if the goal is too abstract, attaining it will never be possible.

It is true that awakening cannot occur without practice—this is a point that karate and Zen meditation have in common.

The technique of karate and the attitude one adopts toward it are based on the presupposition that combat is a matter of life and death. What is in play here is not winning a trophy in competition, but something far more fundamental—our existence in the body within a certain established or expected set of conditions known as combat. Even if you do not engage in actual combat, you must have "combat" as a part of your consciousness in any work with movement.

In okinawa-te, and then in karate, the practice of katas has always been the essence of the training. But in Okinawa, the practitioners were preparing themselves for real confrontations. In addition, there existed a system of duels arising from challenges, which were real fights with a minimum of conventional rules. As a result, techniques of kicking had to be kept within a limited range, because it was essential to safeguard the body as a whole at all times.

In Okinawa and in the initial teachings of the okinawa-te masters who went to Japan, what today is called "free" combat did not exist. For them, it was actual conventional combat. By contrast, today's "free" combat is fighting with controlled movements, which by rule must be halted at the instant of contact with the face or one of the vital points of the opponent. This form of combat was developed in the course of the first period in which karate was taught in the Japanese universities. The intention was to come as close as possible to real combat without causing harm. It was an adaptation of a form of training traditional in kendo (the way of the sword).

Under present circumstances, the opportunity does not exist for us to practice our effectiveness in a concrete way. We are no longer living in the era of duels and single combat. In this situation, the quest for the perfection of effectiveness in karate can occur only in an interiorized fashion. During training, what is important is not scoring points but the quality of mastery of oneself and of the opponent. "Do not win after having struck, but strike after having won."

The criterion for victory is not an external one; the decisive movement does not occur by chance, but is intentional. One has the full experience of one's existence during this movement, which can be perfectly controlled and at the same time not touch the opponent at all. For reaching this point, perfecting physical techniques is only a starting point. In order to make progress, it is necessary to be working in the realm of the mind at the same time that one makes a physical move. The state of awareness that makes possible this form of victory can be compared to a well-polished mirror that reflects reality. This is the point where the work of karate meets the emptiness of Zen. In order to make clear what the combat techniques of karate are, we must constantly bear in mind what their objective is: to achieve the maximum possible effectiveness in bare-handed combat with one or several opponents—that is, in relationship with other people.

Attaining maximal effectiveness in karate means being capable of realizing the full range of one's human effectiveness, which is not qualitatively the same at the age of twenty as it is at forty, nor as it is at eighty, and which always has a twofold composition: technical capacity and psychological state. Seen in this light, the goal of karate does not lie in reaching the highest possible level of physical conditioning, which is necessarily a constantly changing, transitory factor. The work here continues throughout one's lifetime, just as it does in the practice of zazen (sitting in silence in the posture of a buddha), which constitutes the essence of Zen.[4]

We will explore this idea more deeply later on through the examples of several early sword masters. I take the way of the sword as an example because it was in relation to this discipline that the way of the samurai, or budo, was developed; and karate cannot be constituted as budo, as Funakoshi tried to do, except by relying on the accomplishments of the martial arts, which reached their high point in the discipline of swordsmanship.

In order to achieve maximal effectiveness in karate, the idea is that any one blow should be sufficient to disable the adversary. However, this objective is obviously not one that can be achieved at the end of one year of karate practice or even at the end of five. The statement Funakoshi is said to have made at the age of eighty is very significant:

I am finally beginning to understand what the face-level block [*jyodan age-uke*] is.

Blows have to be delivered to the adversary's vital points. As we have said, by "vital points" what is meant is the strategic points of the human body as identified by Oriental medicine. These points are numerous and they differ in both quality and characteristics. Whether we are talking about a massage technique or a karate blow, the force, direction, and form of delivery must vary according to which point is being addressed. Enumerating the vital points would not be useful here. In karate, the practitioner learns the location of the vital points at the same time that he or she learns the techniques for the blows to be directed to one or another of them, the results that can be expected from landing such a blow, and how to control it. Beginners start out by learning the vital points of the front and the medial axis of the body, but these are not the only ones.

Under present-day conditions, learning the vital points is not done to aid in the delivery of blows, but to allow for better control during training. This type of knowledge must be accompanied by the highest level of caution. It is often said that, in karate, the extremities—the hands and feet—are like swords or spears. That is not because they become instruments of cutting or piercing but rather because, in their relationship to the vital points, they develop a very high level of effectiveness.

That is why karate can be very effective as a technique of self-defense, even for someone who is not very strong physically. The current trend in karate is to require a great deal of force as well as physical conditions such as flexibility, weight, size, and so on, but this is actually a sign of a decrease in the valuation and the range of effectiveness of the techniques that were traditionally transmitted.

Though it is not our intention here to provide a manual of karate technique, for the sake of those who do not practice karate, we will briefly show the basic positions.

The following should help us to understand what weapons are available to us:

1. Look first at the open hand. The hand, and particularly the part that strikes, must always be in a state of tension.

Nukite: "hand that pierces or cuts through" (four positions, figures 1 to 4)

Fig. 1

Fig. 2

Fig. 3

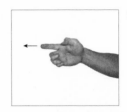

Fig. 4

Shuto: "hand sword," cutting hand (figure 5)

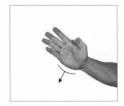

Fig. 5

Haito: cutting hand (figure 6)

Fig. 6

Hai-shu: back of the hand (figure 7)

Fig. 7

Tei-sho: lower end of the palm (figure 8)

Fig. 8

2. Let us now look at the closed hand, first at the hand with the fingers folded back (figure 9).

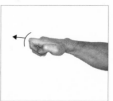

Fig. 9

Hiraken: You strike with the second knuckle of the fingers.

Ipponken: (figures 10, a and b), two positions: you strike with the knuckle of just one finger; there is a variation of this position in which you strike with the knuckles of two fingers joined together.

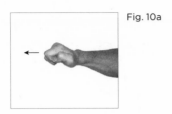

Fig. 10a

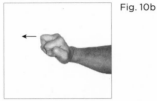

Fig. 10b

Seiken: the tight fist (figure 11). You move to this position from the hiraken position, and you hold the thumb over the index and middle fingers in order to keep the fist well together. You strike with the top two joints of the fingers.

Fig. 11

Tettsui: the hammer fist (figure 12)

Fig. 12

3. Now look at the feet.

Koshi or *josokutei* or *chusoku*: the underside of the foot (figure 13). The foot is held tense with the toes raised; you strike with the end of the sole of the foot.

Teisoku: the sole of the foot
Kakato: the heel

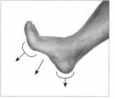

Fig. 13

The top side of the foot (figure 14)
Haisoku: the top of the foot
Tsumasaki: the ends of the toes

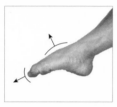

Fig. 14

Outside edge of the foot (figure 15)
Sokuto: "foot sword"

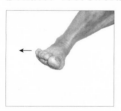

Fig. 15

4. The knee, the elbow, and the head are also capable of delivering blows.

Now let us see what our means of defense are. In karate, in order to block blows, we most often use the hand (in the shuto, haito, hai-shu, and tei-sho positions) with the forearm in different positions; as well as the elbow, the foot (in the teisoku position), and the shin.

Karate is primarily conceived as a means of defense, so attacks only come following a blocking action.[5] Attacks are not studied with the intention of assaulting someone. Thus, parrying or blocking moves play the primary role in karate. But its techniques of defense include techniques of attack.

Tactically speaking, the fundamental sequence is not a block followed by a counterattack, but a block that contains an attack as part of it. For example, during the first stage of the learning process, the practitioner blocks a punch with a concentrated force that breaks the force of the opponent's attack. However, at the same time the intention is also to break his will. By deflecting his force, his energy throws him off balance and shocks him. This causes a momentary gap in his state of mind and makes it possible to follow up with an effective counterattack.

At a more advanced level, the block contains an attack within it already and thus entails immediate domination of the adversary. At this level, the block the karateka uses to protect himself includes a hold by means of which, in deflecting his opponent's force, the karateka either throws him or forces him to the floor. Thus the block is simultaneously an offensive move to which a more violent attack can be added. But very few karatekas reach this level.

It is said that the ultimate stage of karate is one in which there are no punches or kicks; but to reach that level, you must already have worked through the stage of karate that uses punches and kicks. Only the experience of many blocks and attacks integrated into a larger, more sweeping sequence can make possible the level of confidence that requires no punches and no kicks.

Blocks and attacks are executed using the entire body. So even when the movement being studied appears to be only a movement of the arm or the leg, you learn to concentrate and make use of the force of the entire body in this movement.

The goal is to be able to move to defense and attack from any position. However, during the learning period, you begin training on the basis of highly codified positions, often working in the low posture (with the legs bent) in order to strengthen your muscles.

Karate movements are not an extension of the movements of everyday life. To begin with, it is necessary to forge your weapons, that is, to learn to execute the arm techniques of attack and defense and then the techniques for the feet. You must learn to execute them perfectly from the point of view of form as well as to execute them with force while linking these two together. The basic techniques involved here (*kihon*) are numerous. There are punches and kicks that are direct, circular, penetrating, or whip-like.

In Japan it is said that to be able to execute a direct blow of the fist takes three years of training, but for such a punch to become truly effective, ten years are necessary. Therefore two distinct stages must be distinguished here: learning the techniques and learning their uses—in other words, finding out how to make use of your weapons. The use of the techniques is learned by means of katas, which are sequences of movements. Even though you practice katas by yourself, they always presuppose the presence of one or more adversaries.

The fundamental idea of the kata is that while executing them the karateka has to imagine in front of him the adversary toward whom his blows and parries are directed. However, a kata is not simply a piece of mimed combat; it is also a formalization of the techniques of combat that are being transmitted and must be learned.

We should add here that the katas are not always transparent, because, as stated earlier, they were originally designed with the additional need in mind of disguising the intentions of the movements from oppressors or adversaries. Often in the katas, although the technical movements are obvious, their tactical significance for combat remains hidden. This is why insight is necessary to achieve progress by means of the katas. Mere repetition is not enough.

Each style of karate makes use of thirty or forty katas. Since the various styles represent only moderately differentiated developments from a common origin, their relatedness is not hard to see.

2

BUDO AND KARATE GOSHIN-DO

THE THEORY OF BUDO is still in a rudimentary stage of development, especially the theory of bare-handed budo, of which karate-do is a part.

WHAT IS BUDO?

This is a brief definition: budo is a discipline that integrates practical techniques of combat (bu) with a way of life (do) developed by the warrior order of the Japanese feudal period. It is not a mere combination of the two concepts *bu* and *do*, but a dialectical integration of two lines of practice that present a number of contradictory elements.

Bu is generally translated by English words such as "warrior," "military," and "martial arts"; and *do* is translated by such terms as "path," "way," and "discipline." As a body of practices, bu was developed and elaborated along with the development of weapons as fabricated objects and also the techniques for their utilization.

During the time of the warriors, the weapons in use were various kinds of swords, spears, bows, and so on, but it is not the weapon types that define the qualities of budo. It would be a mistake to conceive of budo as a mere technical evolution of bu. It is when bu as such has been qualitatively transcended through its relationship with do that we can begin to speak of budo.

Before examining the notion of do, it seems necessary to reiterate the fact that budo originated in the milieu of the warrior order and developed over a long historical period. It was amended, transformed, experimented upon, and improved not just by one man but by successive generations of warriors. It took on its finished form in the course of the last period of Japanese feudalism. I speak of "finished form" because, in our new social context, we can no longer participate in qualitative development following the same line of evolution.

What we can do is to adapt budo to our times, reconstituting an equivalent form of it that is suited to present-day society. Today, no one lives like the warriors of old. The highest level of budo is now extremely difficult to attain. The masters who did reach this level before the end of the feudal period did so by learning through actual experience; but they also had the benefit of being able, through a process of directly transmitted traditional practice, to avoid mistakes that had been corrected through trial and error over time. They had the added advantage over current practitioners in that their budo was deeply influenced by the way of life and prevailing values of their period. But even under these conditions, masters of budo were very few, and apprenticeship through actual experience was a highly selective process.

At the present time, because of the gap between budo and everyday life, it has become much more difficult, indeed impossible, to attain this supreme level in the manner of the masters of old—by the empirical method, that is, by learning from actual experience. In order to provide it with a new theoretical foundation, we have to relate to budo as it comes down to us today, along with the level of perfection that it reached, and to analyze it in a dialectical

fashion, bringing to the surface the contradictions that exist between the budo of the past and our own social praxis. Then we
must seek to discover what level of development is possible within
our new social context.

Let us take a simple example. Before and after a training ses-
sion, warriors bowed to the altar of the Shinto gods. Now we continue to bow, even if there is no altar to the gods; and some Muslims
who practice the martial arts address this bow to Allah.

The Notion of Do Pervades Various Aspects of Japanese Culture

In Japanese, the word *karate* is often accompanied by the word *do*,
giving us the expression *karate-do*.

This notion of do applies not only to the traditional martial
arts, such as the way of the bow (*kyudo*), the way of the Japanese
sword (kendo), judo, aikido, and so on, but also to other cultural
arts, such as flower arrangement (*kado*), tea ceremony (*sado*), calligraphy (*shodo*), and others. Indeed the idea exists in Japanese
culture that all of the arts come together on a certain level of pro-
fundity in the same spiritual realm.

Furthermore, this realm, which can be attained by means of any
of these disciplines, is the essential element in all the arts. Thorough study of any one of these disciplines is therefore considered
the essential means for bringing one's personal ability to a point
where it is no longer limited to a single area but has expanded to a
universal level applicable to many areas.

A remark by Miyamoto Musashi, a Japanese sword master of
the early seventeenth century, is characteristic of this cultural approach: "I trained every day from morning till night, and it was
when I reached around fifty years of age that I found myself in the
way [do] of strategy of the martial arts." He says this after writing
that he had engaged in combat to the death more than sixty times
in his youth and that he had continuously pursued the study of the
Way. "At this moment, I found myself at the very end of the Way.

And this enabled me to be a master in all of the artistic disciplines." And in fact his works of painting, calligraphy, sculpture, and so forth show that he was an extraordinary artist.

Do is thus conceived of in Japanese culture as a way that leads to a spiritual state in which our human faculties, as expressed in the various realms of the arts, are liberated. The idea is that this spiritual state can be attained through thorough study of any of the artistic disciplines. This notion involves a moral aspect that I will not elaborate upon here beyond saying that in order to follow the Way, it is recommended that one conform to the principles that govern the universe and thus society as well. The process of self-perfection through any single discipline is a process that leads to the realization of the personality as a whole. At this level of realization one is in harmony with the human world as well as with the world of nature.

In order to gain a comprehensive understanding of the notion of do, it would be necessary to study how it is rooted in the system of social relations of the Japanese feudal period and in the collective values of the moral and religious traditions of historic Japan. But such a study is not within the scope of the present book. Here we will examine do only in connection with the practice of the arts.

While, as we have said, the word *do* is usually translated as "way," "path," or "discipline," none of these words catch its entire cultural sense, but rather only something abstract and partial. They express its superficial meaning but entirely miss its deeper content.

As I see it, in the West, there is no system of cultural relations nor any cultural fabric that would make it possible to comprehend the notion of do in depth. The reason is that do is not a mere abstract idea, but rather a moral notion, one that provides orientation and guidance for a way of life. It is a product of historical and social forces that is pervaded by customs, religions, and ancient collective values.

As I have already noted, in the Japanese martial arts introduced into the countries of the West under the name of budo—such as judo, aikido, kendo, karate-do, and kyudo—the notion of do remains on the surface of the discipline as an abstract idea with intellectual ramifications or mystical connotations, while at the same time the physical practice of these martial arts develops within the social framework of sport or as a means of violence. In Japan, by contrast, in spite of a new trend in the direction of sports, the notion of do remains associated with a deeper sense of practice. In Japan it is connected, on the one hand, with certain methods of concentration and physical and psychological force, and on the other, with social norms and models of conduct governing such things as the relations between teachers and students, between more advanced and less advanced students, various forms of courtesy, and so on.

It is true that the larger notion of do has been transmitted to the West and exists as part of the West's image and practice of the Japanese martial arts. However, because of the differences between the Western and Japanese cultures, the real content of this notion has not been communicated. A tendency toward mystification has developed in its place. This often veils inadequacies in mastery of the physical techniques, and is accompanied by authoritarian forms of teacher-student interaction. All this has been said before. My conjecture is that all of this may be evidence of a need to compensate for an absence of value that is felt in present-day Western capitalist societies.

IS KARATE-DO PART OF BUDO?

Let us take a brief historical excursion. It is generally thought that budo reached the high point of its development during the Tokugawa era. This was the final period of domination by the order of warriors, which was marked by a relatively long period of peace among the feudal lords. In the course of this period, budo reached an extraordinary level in the art of swordsmanship, which was a symbol of the order of warriors.

The level attained by the samurai was such that their writings on the sword have been treated as constituting a doctrine, and passages are often quoted with the implication that they contain the truths of budo. However, these writings have never been the subject of scientific study.

It is not merely by chance that karate has produced writings and theories that are much more rudimentary than those produced by the other forms of budo. Karate has only existed under this name for eighty years, despite the very long—and little known—history of bare-handed combat in the East.

Since the purpose of this book is not to provide a history of budo, it is enough for us to note here that despite a widely held idea to the contrary, karate never had its own history as an art of budo, that is, as a cultural production of the warriors of the feudal period. Since its appearance before the public, karate has been included among the arts of budo without ever having been a part of it earlier on in the strict sense of the term. And in contrast to judo and kendo, which began to lose their multidimensional richness as a result of falling under the influence of sport, karate, starting as a simple form of bare-handed combat and drawing strength from the principles of budo, particularly the art of the sword, began partially to absorb the qualities of budo. However, this process has never gone so far as to result in the formulation of a theory.

Definitions remain ambiguous, whether we are talking about the martial arts that are distancing themselves from budo or the martial arts that are coming closer to it.

From its inception on up to the present day, karate continues to be considered by the Japanese public to be on the lowest rank of the qualitative hierarchy of the martial arts—below kendo, kyudo, aikido, judo, and so on. This is not unrelated to the fact that the social status and level of education of the practitioners of karate are very often lower than those of the adepts of the other martial arts.

I believe the explanation for this is as follows. Historically, martial arts such as kendo and kyudo came directly out of the budo of the order of warriors, which occupied the top rank in the feudal social hierarchy. At the beginning of the modern period that came after the Tokugawa era (around 1868), and in spite of the disappearance of the feudal social classes, some of the mental attitudes and collective values of the warriors lived on in the martial arts that were most directly derived from the warrior order. Moreover, the descendants of the order of warriors inherited a proclivity for intellectual work that had developed in the old social context but served them well in relating to the educational system of the new era.[1] Also at the beginning of the modern period, success in one's university career was the condition for a good social position in Japanese society, which was then in the process of transformation to modern capitalism.

The new forms of upward social mobility and the ideology of the formerly dominant warrior class were compatible. This ideological outlook was commonly found among practitioners of kendo and kyudo, who occupied high positions in the capitalistic system of production. The way in which the social position of these men in the new system of production reflected their formerly dominant role as the order of warriors was most acutely felt when they were at the helm of a social group, even a limited one, which was organized on the pattern of "vertical social relations." (This expression refers to chains of hierarchical relations characteristic of contemporary Japanese society. This social pattern has been described well in the work of Chie Nakane entitled, in the English edition, *Japanese Society*.[2])

Aikido, which took shape under that name at the beginning of the twentieth century, has as its goal to dominate one's adversary by shaping one's own forces and movements in accordance with his. The idea is to manipulate the opponent so as to overcome him without a direct clash. That fits perfectly with the ideology of the leaders of businesses or other Japanese social groups organized according to the system of vertical relations. Aikido has many adepts that come from this social stratum.

Karate, by contrast, had no direct connection with the budo of the warriors, although it had been practiced for a long time, particularly in Okinawa. By the beginning of the twentieth century, it had spread throughout Japan, and it was at that time, as we have seen, that it acquired the name *karate*. This word was used for the first time by Master Funakoshi, who soon added to it the suffix *do* in order to bring it closer to *budo*.

The effectiveness of karate as a technique of bare-handed combat was highly appreciated by those who needed to fight for personal reasons or because of their social activities, since bearing arms was strictly prohibited by the new legislation. This is one of the causes for the low esteem in which karate has been held by the Japanese public. To this can be added the relatively low level of education of practitioners of karate, who, again, often come from lower social strata than practitioners of the other martial arts.

Thus karate is situated on the fringes of the martial arts. True, the discipline has given itself the suffix *do*, which continues to bear witness to the intentions of certain karatekas, but no theoretical formulation has come along that, added to the practice itself, would help make a reality out of the *idea* of karate-do.

Whenever elements are introduced from a foreign culture into an existing culture—in this case that of the West—there is a natural tendency to understand them in terms of the elements that already exist in one's own culture. And it so happens that, in the various nations of the West, sport, in its many forms, exercises a dominant influence wherever physical activities are concerned. Budo, which was never introduced in its totality but only in a piecemeal fashion, has been reworked by Westerners into a kind of combat sport. It has attracted a great number of followers thanks to the social network already existing in connection with sports.

There is another aspect of the situation that bears mentioning here. Throughout the development of capitalist societies, it has at times appeared advantageous to employ bare-handed means of violence, that is, those that do not employ firearms. The result has been a twofold strategy that has been adopted toward the martial arts: on the one hand, on the part of repressive apparatuses of the dominant power; and on the other, on the part of certain political factions on the right or the left. The existence of this strategy and the relations martial arts teachers often maintain with the police or other sectors of the state apparatus or the economic establishment has reinforced the position of these teachers and helped them maintain a certain kind of monopoly within the world of sports. The outcome is that it is extremely difficult to really get to the bottom of what is happening in that world, which exposes only its surface—in the form of competitions, matches, training situations, and so on. The world of the martial arts as pervaded by capitalist relationships would be an interesting subject for sociological study, but we shall content ourselves here with a simple reference to the prevailing situation.

BUDO IS NOT A SPORT

In the countries of the West, turning budo into a sport has had the result that it is understood only partially, in general simply as a form of physical expression. However, budo is multidimensional and cannot be understood on this basis. It is therefore important to clarify some fundamental differences between multidimensional budo and one-dimensional budo—differences that are immediately visible on the level of practice.

Some of these differences have been described by the Japanese author Tsugumasa Nango, who contrasts *karate goshin-jutsu* with karate as sport.[3]

Nango's *Budo No Riron* is a unique work from the point of view of the interpretation of budo, especially karate, in spite of the ambiguity of certain terms chosen by the author and the weakness of the theoretical organization of the book. I will examine here the interesting points in his interpretation.

Nango describes two opposing views of karate in order to make clear the importance of choosing one of them from the very beginning of practice. Karate can be understood as (1) a combat or competitive sport; or as (2) *goshin-jutsu*, which can be translated as "techniques of self-defense." The fundamental differences that arise from these two points of view are the following.

First, the result of sports competitions is generally determined, no matter how the match or game works, by the total number of points won by each team or player. This is the case for football, rugby, tennis, and so on. Whatever the content of the match has been, whether it was won by thirty to twenty-nine or by thirty to one, "the winner is the one who has the most points by the end, even if it is only one point more" (quotations are taken from *Budo No Riron*, which has not been translated into English). That means that one can always make up for mistakes made during the match by getting more points. Karate as a competitive sport is no exception to this rule.

The definition of karate as "goshin-jutsu," however, requires a fundamentally different attitude toward mistakes made during practice. Nango writes,

> If you were attacked by someone today and if you lost an eye, it would be futile to declare courageously, "Tomorrow for sure I won't lose it." Once the eye is lost, it can never be won back.

In goshin-jutsu, the essential factor is absolute safety, not the proportion of fights that have been won or lost. The aim is "not losing, and victory in combat is not always the objective. It would have no meaning if, after having won a fight, you were very seriously injured. The fundamental goal is to maintain one's own personal safety."

Second, in a karate sports competition, the object is to win, that is (let us say it again), to score the greatest number of points. Even if your opponent makes the first point, you will still be the winner if you make two points during the remainder of the match. It is very difficult to win in competition if you put the primary emphasis on defense. To win, you must attack. This is what shapes the training system in sports karate. Training is set up to prepare you to score the most possible points. For this reason, there is a tendency to neglect training in those techniques that are not used in competition or in the sports version of karate combat. Moreover, since you only get points for moves recognized by the referees, you are trained only in techniques recognized by the rules referees follow, and your real effectiveness is limited by having to use only techniques that are clearly visible from the outside.

In contrast to that, in karate goshin-jutsu, the referee does not exist. We are not constantly obliged to employ techniques that are visible from the outside. We practice with the presumption that the opponent's attacks might injure us seriously or even kill us. In training, absolute emphasis has to be put on defense, and attack techniques are not always given the highest priority. Since disqualification does not exist, attacks to the vital points, and thus also defense of the vital points, are essential parts of our training.

Third, in the sports form of karate, because of rules that prohibit certain moves or result in penalties, there are many techniques that are considered taboo (attacks to the genitals, the knees, the shins, and so on). As a consequence, these techniques are not in general use, but when, exceptionally, they do come into play, they are worthless for scoring points and often lead to disqualification. Thus these techniques are often omitted from training, and in all likelihood, most sport practitioners of karate do not know them or the means of defending against them.

By contrast, disqualification does not exist in goshin-jutsu. All the vulnerable places or vital points of the human body can be the object of attack. For this reason, training includes learning how to protect them through various techniques of defense and parry. In the practice and training of karate as goshin-jutsu, the approach always taken is that any of the attack techniques employed by the opponent might be lethal. As a result, defense techniques acquire absolute importance.

At the same time, though attack techniques are not learned for the purpose of killing, they must be effective to the point where we could kill with them if we wanted to. Nango tells us,

> The same is true here as in assessing the value of a sword. Even if the sword has a beautiful form, it has no value either from the aesthetic point of view or from the functional point of view if it does not cut well.

In the practice of karate goshin-jutsu, the thought must always exist that every attack could be a lethal one and therefore that a mistake might mean death. This thought is what gives direction to our training and provides the orientation that encourages us to advance toward a certain kind of perfection that differs perceptibly from that pursued by an athlete or the practitioner of a sport. Nango says further,

> In budo practiced in the form of goshin-jutsu, our very life is at stake. "Victory or defeat" is a matter of life or death. The idea that defeat means death is obvious. Karate as a sport, on the other hand, is a mere technical competition in which defeat is not at all connected with the idea of death, even though technical competition might bring on the most serious of accidents.

These fundamental differences between karate goshin-jutsu and karate as a sport lie at the root of differences that characterize the training found in each of them.

With regard to the technical effectiveness of karate goshin-jutsu, every attack technique has as its aim to make possible the death of the adversary (hence the term "killing technique"), and the aim of the defense techniques is to maintain one's own personal safety. But we do not learn the attack techniques with the intention of killing. This means that "the attack techniques can kill if necessary; in this they have the same value as a sword." The value of the sword lies in the unity of its beautiful form and its ability to cut. If one of these is missing, it has no value.

A MULTIDIMENSIONAL DEFINITION OF KARATE: KARATE GOSHIN-DO

Within the framework of Nango's distinction, I agree with the idea of karate goshin-jutsu. But it seems to me important to take a closer look at the term *goshin-jutsu* in order to situate our point of departure clearly. The word *goshin* is composed of *go*, translated as "to protect" or "to defend"; and *shin*, translated as "body," "self," or "man." *Jutsu* means "technique" or "method." So the translation of *goshin-jutsu* would be "set of techniques for human self-defense" or "set of techniques for human defense."

But the term *jutsu* does not take into account a fundamental aspect of budo: budo is multidimensional and in particular has a profound dimension that encompasses various aspects of the martial arts as well as various aspects of the arts of life. It has as its aim the full flowering of our human faculties in a wide variety of different areas. All this is well expressed by the notion of do. For this reason, I define karate as *goshin-do*, which could be partially translated in English as "the way, or path, of bare-handed human defense," or "human self-defense." Thus we are no longer talking about a mere set of techniques. A do leads us into a profound dimension through an expression that takes the form of techniques. A do is multidimensional in its structural composition.

In my view, karate as goshin-do is capable of providing us with an equivalent of budo that is valid in our contemporary social context. The sense in which I am using the word *do* is the one I have defined above, and should not be confused with the special interpretation of *do* found in Taoism.

In this work, I intend to approach the theoretical study of karate defined as goshin-do. I will do this with the aim of developing an interpretation of the practice that will provide a proper basis for the practitioner to make progress to more advanced levels on the Way.[4] It is true that through a mere experiential approach, we can arrive at a level of advancement that accords with our level of skill and other qualities that we possess. But a purely empirical or experiential approach will not enable us to reach the highest level of budo, the level attained by a few warriors of the feudal period. Moreover, by following such a purely empirical or experiential approach, many practitioners will be eliminated from the path that leads to the highest point.

The Overall Structure of Karate Goshin-do

Since karate goshin-do is multidimensional, we cannot establish a method for making progress in it without having clarified its structure. In analyzing bare-handed combat as it is practiced in karate goshin-do, we can distinguish three dimensions: first, the dimension of the physical techniques; second, the dimension of *maai* (which can be partially translated as "distance") and of *hyoshi* (partially translated as "cadence"); and third, the dimension of *yomi* (which can be understood as intuitively anticipating the movements of the adversary or adversaries).

I would define the structure of bare-handed budo as the dynamic and simultaneous synthesis of these three dimensions. If even one of them is missing, bare-handed budo cannot be realized. All three are interdependent and they interpenetrate one another. No one of them is viable without the support of the other two. Each of the three elements presupposes both of the others.

Let us look at this more closely. On the surface of the phenomenon, we find the corporeal dimension, the physical techniques. This dimension is the one that is most observable from the outside. The other two dimensions can only be accessed through this one. Thus it is not without reason that there is a tendency to assimilate bare-handed budo to the sphere of combat sports by reducing it to its physical techniques. This trend has gone farthest in Western countries, where the image of budo has been caught up in the cultural web of the sports world.

Particularly at the beginning of the process of learning barehanded budo, it can seem that the physical techniques are everything. It is not until the student reaches a certain level in his learning of the physical techniques that we can even begin to speak of bare-handed budo. But there are obstacles to reaching this point. The learning process here can be compared to getting through a tough shell, a barrier that surrounds the most highly developed form of bare-handed budo. In order to get through this shell, the student needs a kind of orientation that will make him aware of the existence of other aspects of his development. Such an orientation may well be lacking. In such a case, even if he has attained a level where it should be possible for him to get through the shell, he is unable to do so—he is unable to enter the realm of bare-handed budo in its totality because he lacks the tools of the second two dimensions.[5] This is the current situation with regard to barehanded budo in the countries of the West, where practitioners remain stuck in the first dimension: the physical techniques. They remain stuck in karate as a sport—that is saying the same thing.

Another question is that of physical ability. It goes without saying that physical ability is very important for getting into budo altogether, but in the long run, it is not an indispensable condition. In general, those with good physical abilities quickly become effective up to a certain level, but one sees that they often have a tendency to depend too much on their physical talent. Without truly having gotten through the shell mentioned above, they think that because they have made such rapid progress, they are headed in the right direction. Thus they are inclined to continue on the same track, paying no attention to the existence of the second two dimensions.

Basically, progress in budo occurs in the integrated development of the three dimensions that begins after having passed through the first—physical technique—phase we have just been talking about. The level of advancement of a practitioner of bare-handed budo can be determined by the way in which he has integrated the three dimensions. Thus the principle that guides our method of advancement must be development of each of the dimensions in itself and in its simultaneous integration with the two others.

The bare-handed budo of a lad of twenty in good physical condition is based for the most part on his efficiency in the use of his bodily force. If he is not oriented toward multidimensional progress, his effectiveness will decrease when he reaches a certain age, in direct proportion to the deterioration of his physical condition. This depends on his strength and muscular stamina, on his flexibility, the speed of his reflexes, and so on.

The other two dimensions, maai and hyoshi together, and yomi, do not develop in the same way as the physical techniques do. My own practice, my observations, and the documents I have consulted show that these two dimensions do not diminish with age. Rather, they continue to develop, and their further deepening occurs in conjunction with that of the first dimension.

An elderly budo master—a master of kendo, aikido, or karate-do—can easily defeat younger students. From the outside, it looks like he wins by using his feet and his hands, but his movements are only the visible result of his considerable superiority in the other two dimensions of budo. This makes his movements extremely effective. This is very difficult to perceive from the outside, because a sufficiently seasoned eye is necessary to see it. For those who are incapable of seeing in depth, beyond mere movements, the combats they watch will perhaps be disappointing, because they are often not at all spectacular. And even when they look impressive, the most spectacular moments are not the ones that are truly effective. Combats between young fighters often seem much more dynamic, given the fact that the show is made up of movements that manifest on the most superficial, which is to say the most apparent, of levels. In that case, the effect achieved is the direct result of spectacular moves. But a win of this sort is no real indication of the quality of the combatant.

Spectacular combat moves, such as leaps and big kicks and punches, are often due to a lack of precision; thus such movements are not necessary.

This being the case, it must be admitted that elderly masters might not necessarily be capable of playing a showy role in karate films. What counts in these films is spectacular, often acrobatic, moves, which are intended to directly communicate an impression of power to spectators via the screen. The superficial, large-scale movements that convey this impression most easily often prevent spectators from going through the mental process necessary to understand the less obvious phenomena of combat. This is where the distinction between a film star and a genuine adept of the martial arts gets lost.

If we, as observers or participants, place importance only on the external aspect—the form aspect of combat—we will never be able to grasp what the force possessed by elderly masters is. Thus their victories will seem improbable and will either become the object of some mystical interpretation or will be denied altogether as a deception.

We are now in a better position to understand the meaning of the formulation of Takano Sazaburo, sword master of the nineteenth century, when he said, "Don't win after having struck, but strike having won." Delivering a blow is a simple movement of the body. A win in budo is not brought about by a chance movement. One has to create a situation of combat that goes beyond vagueness and uncertainty. When we win in maai, hyoshi, and yomi, our movement of attack signifies absolute victory. We strike "after having won." This is the aim of training in budo.

Miyamoto Musashi distinguished two ways of winning: (1) the one we have just described, winning with certainty; and (2) winning as a result of a series of fortuitous coincidences. Musashi, an impassioned adept of the way of *ken* (the sword), made the statement that it is necessary for each stroke of the sword to be so effective that it can kill an adversary even if it strikes by chance.

Nevertheless, it is obvious that budo training must be directed toward developing the ability to "strike after having won." That means it must be directed toward integration of the three dimensions of budo.

We will now examine each of these three dimensions.

We will begin with the dimension of physical technique, because that is the one that is on the surface of the phenomenon of bare-handed budo. Then, moving in the direction of the more subtle and the more elusive, I will undertake to describe the dimension of maai and hyoshi; and finally that of yomi.

This will enable us to understand the sword matches often talked about in Japan in which two high-level adversaries fight and conclude their match without ever having exchanged a blow. The match has taken place on the levels of maai and hyoshi and of yomi. One of the combatants understands that he has lost without even being struck. The other one sees that he has won without ever having had to launch his attack; or else, in some cases, without having exchanged blows, both combatants acknowledge that they are evenly matched and have reached a draw.

3

THE DIMENSION OF PHYSICAL TECHNIQUE

THE TWO ASPECTS OF PHYSICAL TECHNIQUE: FORM AND FORCE

In bare-handed budo, especially in karate goshin-do, the physical techniques can be divided into two aspects: (1) the techniques considered from the point of view of form, for example, the specific form of punches and kicks, of blocks, of movements from place to place, of holds, and of falls; and (2) the physical techniques considered from the point of view of developing force—the effectiveness factor.

In practice these two are often inseparable, but this distinction seems necessary to me since this dimension is the first stage of practice and varies considerably according to the different types of practitioners: children, adults, the elderly. Each group's physical condition is different, and so are their motivations and the length of their practice sessions. The teaching of physical techniques must take into account all these differences.

For example, children can learn the form aspect of the techniques—the different kinds of punches and kicks—with relative ease. However, this does not mean that they have learned all there is to know about the physical techniques, because the immature state of their bodies makes it dangerous for them to learn about force. Therefore their techniques cannot truly be effective. For that, they have to reach the age where maturity has ripened and balanced their bodies. Then they will be able to work with force without risk of accident or disturbance of their growth pattern.

By contrast, some adults who are in very good physical condition can realize their effectiveness, within certain limits, before having really learned the form of the techniques perfectly.

In order better to explain the difficulties encountered in learning the form aspect of the physical techniques of bare-handed budo, particularly karate goshin-do, let us take the well-known example of classical dance. The gestures and movements in classical dance are not a direct extension of the movements people make in everyday life. They are the result of perfections in technique developed gradually over the course of an historical period devoted to creating an aesthetic experience through the medium of the human body in motion. They constitute a gestural repertoire that is different from that of everyday life and that is the subject of a special learning process. What is being taught to dance students today is the crystallization of a historical formalization of physical techniques.

The same is true of bare-handed budo, regarded from the point of view of form. It is the result of the accumulated effort of warriors over the whole course of the feudal period, effort devoted toward attaining effectiveness in combat. Here, too, the result is a formalization of physical techniques that are not an extension of the ordinary movements of everyday life. This has turned out to be the main difficulty students encounter in trying to learn the techniques of karate goshin-do, where in addition to learning the forms, the movements must be imbued with force.

KIME: ULTIMATE DECISIVENESS

In karate goshin-do, maximal effectiveness of the physical techniques is expressed by the term *kime*, which can be translated as "ultimate decisiveness."

The notion of *kime* contains two ideas: (1) perfection in the form of a movement; and (2) a level of force heightened to the limit.

The first of these two elements is present not only in the martial arts but also in a variety of Japanese cultural practices that include at least a minimal amount of physical movement, such as classical Japanese dance and theater, the tea ceremony, calligraphy, flower arranging, and so on.

During the performance of these arts, there are a number of points at which perfection of physical form becomes key. Such physical expressions manifest as a momentary pause in the course of a single continuous harmonious movement. This momentary pause, if I may put it this way, corresponds to a condensation of time that brings together the person who makes the gesture either with the space surrounding him or her (for example, the stage in the case of dance or theater), or with the objects that are being created (e.g., the tea, the flower arrangement, the calligraphy).

In such decisive moments, the performer must feel precisely identified with the movement he is making. He must feel that he exists completely in this act, without separation. There must be no thought of a self as an acting subject, no sense of the intention of an acting self, not even a sensation of self. The movement, the object, and the self must form an indivisible whole.

The short pause in the movement marks an extremely dense moment, a moment that concentrates the process of artistic expression that has just taken place. The fruition of the tea ceremony, for example, is not just the act of drinking the tea but the experience of "tasting" the entire process as, in its unfolding, it defines a time and a space.

The second element of kime, force, is unique to budo, where it plays the role of making each technical movement an effective one. Kime reaches its maximal point when the physical form is fully executed with the element of force it can contain heightened to the limit.

In karate goshin-do, kime in punches and kicks can be realized once a certain level of accomplishment has been reached, but the quality of the kime will vary according to the real level of the kara-tekas, from kime of a low level to kime of a high level. In fact the physical techniques in karate goshin-do are the equivalent of the sword in kendo, for the quality of the sword itself can range from mediocre to superb.

Thus in the first dimension of budo, once we succeed in realizing kime in the physical techniques, our efforts should be directed toward a higher level of performance with regard to both form and force. Success here can be likened to having the best-quality sword, well-sharpened.

The role of force in kime has been the subject of a considerable amount of confusion. For this reason, I will go into further detail on this point, taking the example of an average adult.

It is a well-known fact that the muscular force that we can normally put out in our ordinary state of mind does not represent the absolute limit of our power. It might even be said that we are not capable of exerting our muscular force to the limit in our ordinary state of mind.

There is a mental threshold that governs our ability to make our muscles function at their full potential strength. If we develop ourselves to go beyond this threshold in a particular situation, we will be able put out much more strength than is possible in everyday life. To understand this better, let us take two examples.

First, it is well known that in life-or-death circumstances—for instance, a fire or some other situation that presents unexpected danger—people become capable, without realizing it, of feats of strength that go beyond their usual ability. In Japan, the case has often been observed of women carrying precious pieces of furniture out of a fire, and then later, after calm has returned, proving incapable of moving any of them, much to their amazement. There is even a Japanese popular expression drawn from this phenomenon: "the enormous, mad strength of being in the midst of flames."

Second, there is a simple experiment that is often performed in sessions of hypnosis. An ordinary hypnotized person who has been told to tense his body can maintain a totally horizontal position with his body suspended without being supported in any other way than by a chair placed under his head and another chair under his feet. Under hypnosis, such a person lying suspended between two chairs can even support the weight of another person sitting on his belly. But once he has returned to his ordinary psychological state, he can no longer do these things. In such cases, we can see that there is a psychological threshold that prevents the human body from functioning at its top strength, a threshold that helps maintain mental and physical balance.

My hypothesis is that kime, which entails having our strength heightened to its maximum level, can only be realized by going beyond this threshold at certain selected moments during the execution of a technique. The process of executing the technique can function as an inner stimulus that pushes us beyond the threshold. At the moment that the technical form reaches the point of kime, our force will be raised above and beyond the ordinary threshold.

To understand this further, let us consider two aspects of training, through repetition, in a simple technique, for example, a punch. The first goal of the training is to automatize the correct execution of the movement, from the point of view of both form and force. The second is to channel the sensation of the physical movement in such a way that it becomes a stimulus for going beyond the force threshold. In my view, what we are doing here is creating new psychophysical, or neural, networks that are not formed in the course of everyday physical activities. This second side of the training is often overlooked.

The *kiai* cry let out by someone executing a movement functions as a self-stimulus in the form of a sound. Such a cry can create a psychological state that enables the karateka to go beyond the force threshold. At the same time, the exhalation caused by the abdominal contraction produced at the moment of the kiai acts as an internal physical stimulus for the concentration of force. Here we see the very important role played in budo by coordination of breath and movement. The kiai is a kind of concentrated breath that makes it possible to augment the force of a particular chosen movement. On the whole, this cry can have different functions, depending on whether it is directed toward oneself, toward one's adversary or adversaries, or toward both at the same time. We will return to these points later on.

Training aimed at developing force in karate goshin-do must focus on this coordination of breath and movement with the goal of going beyond the force threshold.

In studying the development of force in karate goshin-do, an objective examination of the force threshold in connection with the process of kime seems to me essential. We must look at the psychological and physical state that is present at the moment of going beyond the threshold. The existence of kime has been confirmed in years past by adepts of different traditional forms of budo, but no experimental study has been done up to the present time. Carrying out such a study would require a collaboration of different branches of the sciences working in conjunction with karate practitioners who have been guided by an objective theory.

I shall now present my own hypotheses on this point. They are based on my personal experience, but for the moment, in the absence of systematic studies, they must remain only hypotheses.

First, in order to practice kime on the highest level, it is obviously necessary to have a body in sufficiently solid condition to be able to undertake continuous training in karate goshin-do. Solid physical condition of this sort is something that can be developed over the course of a long initial training period; it is not absolutely necessary in order to begin. This particular kind of physical solidity is the kind that makes it possible to carry out the techniques. It has precise characteristics that are not those of just any body that is in good shape. This solidity must be developed in tandem with developing skill in the techniques.

Force in karate is not always proportional to muscle size. It also incorporates a quality of resistance in the various parts of the body—namely, the muscles, the bones, the joints, the nervous system, the intestines, and so on—when the practitioner executes punches and kicks, for example, or other movements at high speed. This kind of conditioning is indispensable for being able to reach the force threshold. This refers to the *ascending phase*, approaching the threshold from below.

Second, when we come back from kime to below the threshold, we need sufficient physical solidity to retain a state of balance as we absorb the consequences of a drop in force inside our body in returning to normal conditions after having gone beyond them. This refers to the *descending phase*.

Normally, these two aspects of physical solidity would be acquired simultaneously in the course of training, but it seems important to me to distinguish them in the framework of experimental research.

THE DEFINITION OF PROGRESS IN TRAINING

By way of concluding this chapter, let me again summarize my hypotheses aimed at establishing the main outlines of a system for progress in training.

In the dimension of physical technique in karate goshin-do, the principal objective is to achieve the highest level of kime. Kime has two aspects: form and force.

As to the first, we should learn the form of the techniques that have been transmitted to us as correctly as possible. We should choose the most highly perfected form of a given technique that has been reached over the course of history. Personal evolution in relation to the formal techniques cannot be envisaged until after the practitioner has reached the point of being able to apply force in kime by means of a technique that he has acquired in its correct form.

As to the second, our efforts must be directed toward going beyond a threshold that is at once physical and mental. In order to do that, we must develop the force and physical solidity that will allow us both to go beyond the threshold (ascending phase) and to maintain our inner balance when, once more below the threshold, the force drops off (descending phase). At the same time, we must orient our mental state toward going beyond the threshold by working on the breath (in particular, the kiai) and on our physical movements.

On this point, I can only say that, on the basis of my limited personal study of the matter, kime is an instantaneously arising mental condition in which there is no consciousness of self and no thought. That is, there is a kind of mental emptiness that totally integrates the self with a given physical movement. The self that executes the movement penetrates completely into it, and dissolves for a very short instant into this physical gesture.

By way of concluding this section, here is an anecdote that seems to me to illustrate in a striking fashion what kime in the martial arts really is.

Kenkichi Sakakibara (1830–1894) was a master of the sword who lived at the end of the Tokugawa period, when the shoguns were in power, and the beginning of the Meiji era. During the period of transition, at the time of the conflicts that led to the overthrow of the power of the shoguns, the principal weapons in use were the sword in urban combat and the rifle in pitched battles. The level of accomplishment of the swordsmen of this period was very high. The techniques that had been interiorized and retransmitted for two hundred and fifty years of peace among the feudal lords now suddenly came into use on a grand scale.

However, in the aftermath of this revolution, starting with the onset of the modern period in 1868, the martial arts, including that of the sword, underwent a major loss of status, and at the same time, the warriors lost their privileges, while priority was given to modernization of the army.

Sakakibara continued in the lifestyle of a master of the sword throughout this period. He remained socially isolated as he continued to pursue perfection in his art, with which he more or less completely identified his existence. Despite the legal prohibitions, he continued for a long time to carry his sword and wear the topknot of a samurai. In 1887, a demonstration of *kabuto wari* (*kabuto* means "steel helmet"; *wari* means "to cut") was organized in honor of the Meiji emperor by one of the emperor's relatives. Sakakibara, who was then fifty-seven years old, was invited to participate in this demonstration along with two other masters who were considered to be among the best. Kabuto wari consisted in slashing a helmet with a sword. The helmet was made by hand from particularly resistant steel meant to repel attacks from swords, spears, and even bullets. Although such helmets were generally considered to be impervious to a sword stroke, a number of stories related that certain exceptional warriors had succeeded in killing their enemy by cutting through their helmet with a sword.

Sakakibara, who was informed of this demonstration a month in advance, tried cutting through a few helmets, but with no success. Each time, the sword bounced off with a metallic sound, leaving the blade damaged or twisted. The day of the demonstration came. He had decided to commit suicide by hara-kiri if he did not succeed. He entrusted his fate to the god of the martial arts, telling himself that it was impossible to execute kabuto wari through human power alone. A helmet of the highest quality had been furnished for the demonstration. The two masters who preceded Sakakibara failed in their attempts to cut into it, leaving not a mark on the helmet. The first one's sword rebounded with a sharp clang, while the sword of the second glanced off the metal. Sakakibara bowed to the emperor, then meditated before the helmet, never averting his gaze from it. Then he gently raised his sword. When he felt filled with ki, he struck with a kiai—"*Ei!*" The helmet did not move, but the sword of the blade had penetrated it. The helmet had a ten-and-a-half-centimeter (over four-inch) gash in it, but there was not a mark on the blade of the sword.

4

THE DIMENSIONS OF
MAAI AND HYOSHI

THE MOMENT OUR CONCEPTION of karate goes beyond the dimension of physical technique, we enter into the perspective of karate goshin-do, and we can take a step forward by using multidimensional techniques. From this point on, we must distinguish two fundamentally different stages: the stage of learning the physical techniques and the stage of using them.

The first stage corresponds to the point where we acquire a way of working with our body that gives us the equivalent of a sword; but at this stage we have not yet learned how to use this sword. Here we acquire the punches and the kicks with which we can knock out or even kill an opponent, but this still involves only a one-dimensional learning process. Having completed this first stage is like the moment in kendo when a beginner takes up a real cutting sword but does not yet know how to use it properly.

At the same time that we are learning how to develop physical techniques that are increasingly effective (or, by analogy, to sharpen the blade of the sword), we must learn how to use them against an opponent. We must practice the physical techniques in relation to

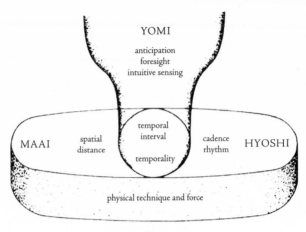

YOMI

anticipation
foresight
intuitive sensing

temporal
interval

MAAI   spatial
distance   temporality   cadence
rhythm   HYOSHI

physical technique and force

Fig. 17
The Relationship of the Three Dimensions

the adversary in the dimensions of maai and hyoshi and of yomi. In this way, it is possible to reach the apex of development in the multidimensional structure that has been shown us by past masters of the art.

The second dimension contains two overlapping, interpenetrating elements, maai and hyoshi. We can portray them schematically as two intersecting circles (see diagram above).

THE NOTION OF MAAI

The word *maai* is usually translated as "distance." In fact, in the literal sense, it is composed of the word *ma*, which means not only "distance" or "interval (between objects) in space," but also "an interval in time"—the moment in music where the rhythm changes, and so on; and of the verb *ai*, which means "a meeting of two or several persons or objects." Thus the word *maai*, in addition to the abstract idea of distance or interval, expresses a movement of getting closer or moving farther apart in relation to persons or objects. In practice, maai is inseparable from hyoshi, as it also is from the dimension of yomi.

1. Maai among the Japanese Sword Masters

The sword adepts of the Japanese feudal period often emphasized the importance of maai: "The most important thing in combat is ma."[1] Either way, whether the adversary or myself is attacking or defending, "it is the accuracy of ma that determines the result of the combat," as the seventeenth-century master Ito Ittosai said.

To illustrate the notion of maai, I will take the pertinent example of the technique of *muto* (*mu* means "without," and *to* means "sword"). The sword master Yagyu Munenori (1571–1646) wrote the following in *Heiho Kaden Sho*, a book that conveyed his particular family tradition of the practice of swordsmanship:

The technique of muto is the one used when one does not have a sword in hand in order to avoid being killed by sword attack.

To achieve this, the master grabs hold of the sword that his opponent is attacking him with. In this way, the sword attached to the hands of the enemy becomes his own sword, and the tables are turned. Thus he does not need to have a sword in hand in order to fight.

When the moment comes to fight bare-handed against a sword, "he can always use whatever he finds around him: a simple fan, a small cane, [etc.] to render the sword attacks ineffective." The point is that he is not dependent on a weapon in the form of a particular object to fight against one or more swords, but he must possess very great skill in combat, even beginning from a situation where he is caught bare-handed. To do that, as Yagyu Munenori says, "one must know the ma [maai] at which the enemy's sword will touch me or not touch me."

Through controlling the ma, the warrior will always be capable of avoiding an enemy's attack by unfailingly maintaining only three centimeters' (a little more than an inch) distance between his body and the blade of the sword. Inside this ma (closer to the adversary in space and time), he must make use of the muto technique. This is only applicable at distances and at moments when the blade of the enemy can reach him. "Knowing the ma well, I let the blade of the enemy's sword cut the air up to just before it reaches my body, then block the movement of the sword handle, since that does not cut." And he adds, "I rip the sword away from him if necessary."

The technique of muto resulted from challenging the validity of the way of the sword as such. For an adept of the sword such as Munenori, who had been found to be superior to all the other swordsmen of his era, the question had to arise of how he would fight if he were not carrying a sword. Was his superiority as a fighter dependent solely on an object, his sword? For a person like Munenori, who sought to perfect his art to the limit, any dependence on an object had to be transcended. He had no choice but to go back to the starting point, his bare hands. How would he be able to defend himself without a weapon against sword-bearing enemies attacking him with intent to kill? It was in response to this question that he developed the technique of muto.

However, we cannot gain a clear idea of this technique from Munenori book, which does not explain it in detail, but rather only gives instructions intended for adepts who had already attained a certain level of the Way and were therefore capable of assimilating them.

This muto technique is analogous in its multidimensional mastery to a phenomenon I described at the beginning of this book whereby an older master of the Japanese martial arts can often easily and faultlessly defeat young students. Yagyu's approach provides us with a fairly complete example of how progress is made in budo.

Although Yagyu mentions only the word *ma* in his book, ma is strongly pervaded by hyoshi and yomi at the same time that it is underpinned by the dimension of physical techniques and physical force. But in accordance with the custom of authors of his period, he does not explicitly spell out the sword techniques in their entirety; rather readers are expected to grasp them by deciphering

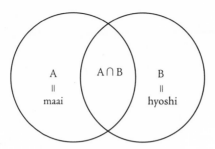

A = maai = spatial distance
B = hyoshi = cadence and rhythm
AB (common to A and B) = temporal interval
during which awareness lags behind in its
relation to physical movement.

Fig. 16

key images that become intelligible on the basis of each reader's own progress on the Way. It is impossible to execute muto without relying on one's sense of maai.

2. The Maai of Space: The Distance between Two Combatants

For the sake of our exploration, let us imagine two bare-handed combatants confronting each other in karate goshin-do combat. We can observe the maai from the outside as a distance between the combatants that varies with the movements of each of them; and in these changes of distance we can distinguish certain rhythms of getting closer and farther away. For the moment, let us leave aside the maai as an interval in time. The temporal interval involves maai, hyoshi, and yomi at the same time. It is a sort of meeting point of those two dimensions.

The maai of space is a phenomenon of the distance between the two combatants. To grasp this aspect more clearly, one must first eliminate a dead-end logical argument that is sometimes put forward here. According to this, in a combat between two persons who are more or less on the same level of accomplishment, the one with the longest limbs has the best chance of winning, and when this difference becomes sufficiently great, it is almost impossible for the smaller man to win.

This logic might be valid for people who practice karate in just one dimension; or it might also apply to beginners who are still just learning the physical techniques. For it is true that at first glance, the external manifestation of karate appears to be a matter of delivering punches and kicks. This view is based on the physical determinism associated with sports. It is further reinforced by the weight categories in judo, which are based on the presumption that a heavy person has the advantage over a lighter one. These categories are an upshot of the fact that judo has ceased to be multidimensional, having been transformed into a one-dimensional combat sport. If one continues to regard combat from the point of view of physical determinism, the following saying, which is very well known among practitioners of the Japanese martial arts, that "the small can defeat the big, and flexibility can overcome force" becomes a mere expression of myth. If one were to take this view to the extreme, one could replace the technical learning process with mere weight gain.

Thus as far as distance in combat is concerned, first of all we have to do away with this dead-end logic so that we can overcome the prejudice that a small combatant cannot defeat a big one.

So our first observation in this context is that for those who enter the multidimensional practice of karate goshin-do, length of limb is not a principal factor in mastering the element of distance.

The Conception of an Attack from the Point of View of Range

Without taking the time to describe the different kinds of attack, let us go directly to the example of a straight-ahead punch as a means of explaining the notion of range of attack in karate goshin-do.

At first glance, it appears evident that somebody who has long arms can reach farther with his punch than somebody with short arms. But this is not always the case.

For those who have mastered the first dimension of karate, the very conception of what kicks and punches are comes to include further intensity and to entail a much greater range than it does for beginners who are still learning the first dimension. For beginners, a punch, for example, is conceived of as a blow struck by suddenly extending the arm with the fist closed. Punches can be delivered at any point in the process that consists of extending the arm until it is straight. Thus the range of the punch is determined by the length of the arm.

But for those who have reached the second stage, punches can also be delivered after the arm has been completely extended forward.

Thanks to a muscular contraction that preserves proper form and thanks to the force brought to bear by kime, of which we have spoken in the previous chapter, advanced practitioners can deliver an effective punch by moving the body forward with the arm tensed and maintained in a state of kime. It is as though they had in front of them a solid piece of wood in the form of the arm held firmly in front of the chest with which they are moving forward for the attack. In certain circumstances this kind of punch is more effective than a punch delivered as one is extending one's arm. It goes without saying that such a punch is only possible after having acquired a high degree of kime in working with the dimension of physical technique.

One of the reasons that length of limb does not entirely determine effective distance is the relativity of these two kinds of attack. A large combatant can strike farther with a punch by extending his arm without moving his body forward (in the second stage, this type of punch has to be delivered with kime), whereas a smaller combatant can deliver a punch with his arm tensed in kime from a shorter distance and also at long distance by moving his body forward, with both situations presenting different advantages. The rapidity of the repetition and sequencing of blows also varies from one person to another, and often rapidity is facilitated for small combatants by the very fact that their limbs are shorter, and this tends to counterbalance the bigger combatant's advantage of longer reach in the simple punch.

It is, however, true that in competition, where attacks can only be above the belt and no attacks are allowed to the legs other than sweeps, a larger combatant has an advantage. But in training for self-defense combat, where all parts of the body are potential objects of attack and thus also of defense, when a taller person takes the combat posture, although his head and torso are relatively less accessible for a smaller opponent, his long legs present an easier target for attack (by kicks to the knees, the shins, or the thighs).

In sum, since the effectiveness of punches between two combatants results from the multifaceted relativity of force, speed, body balance, choice of techniques,[2] and mental state, all in the course of movement through space in time, we cannot judge on the face of it whether a larger or smaller combatant has the advantage as far as distance in combat is concerned.

Nevertheless, speaking of kicks or punches in isolation is an oversimplification. In a combat situation, punches presuppose kicks and kicks presuppose punches.

Distances: Inside and Outside the Boundaries of the Range of Attack

Around the body of a person, at the level of the navel, we can imagine a circle beyond which none of this person's attacks can hit their target, but within which at least one of his various attack moves can be effective. This limited range is proportional not only to the person's size, but also to his level of progress in the dimension of physical techniques. In general, it can be said that in the course of the process of learning the physical techniques, a person reaches a range limit that is on the low side of what he is capable of, and then in the course of further progress, that range will reach its maximum extent.

Thus, when we reach the stage of applying the techniques, we have a certain definite maximum range; and this range will begin to diminish along with our physical force beginning at a certain age. But this diminution will be counterbalanced by development in the other two dimensions, as long as our work on the Way is properly oriented.

I will now examine the progress of practitioners who have really mastered the physical techniques and who are therefore capable of reaching the second stage. Nowadays there are only a few practitioners who meet this criterion. Within the circular line representing their range limit, these practitioners have at their disposal at least one technique that will be effective at any distance from their body within this range. This could refer to punches, kicks, elbow or knee blows, head butts, throws, holds, and so on.

It goes without saying that the attacks of two persons in combat will only be effective within the range limit of each of them and will be ineffective beyond it. Thus at the beginning of the combat, the two persons will be separated by a distance that is greater than the longer of their two range limits.

The range limit does have a relationship with a combatant's length of limb, but that relationship is not constant. Moreover, it is not necessarily the case that the combatant with the longest reach always has the advantage.

Conditions of an Effective Attack;
Moments of Vulnerability

In karate goshin-do, a man's hands and feet are the equal of a sword only at the moment they are being used in the application of specific techniques. For them to become a weapon, they have to have a sufficient energy charge and be making a specific motion. The sword, as an object, always has the capacity to cut, but a man's hand is only a hand. It cannot have a cutting quality unless it is being charged with energy by a movement, and this requires technique, cadence, and mental concentration.

In other words, a man's hand or foot can become a weapon during a very brief time span, which corresponds to the coordination of technique and mental concentration brought to their very highest level. This rules out an approach that envisages blows landing by chance. That is why in traditional kendo training, a shout, or kiai, is used to mark the instant of a blow and the part of the opponent's body that is going to be hit.

It must be emphasized that a combatant's punch or kick never functions like a piston that moves along its trajectory with constant force. In the attack trajectory, the hand only functions as a weapon at the instant corresponding to coordination just mentioned; this only represents a small part of the movement the hand makes. In the movement of a distance attack (punch or kick), there is always a rather large preparatory part of the trajectory, which is a necessary part of the makeup of the attack. Generally speaking, the longer the range of the attack, the longer this preparatory part of its trajectory has to be.

Moreover, when one attacks, the intent to attack precedes the movement. That is to say, one projects one's intent to the point one wishes to strike before the attack gets there. This lag occurs in the course of the preparatory movement of the attack, and this appears to the experienced eye of an opponent on the level of the second stage as a moment of vulnerability both in the form and in the force of the attack. This means that in the preparatory phase of the trajectory of an opponent's attack he can spot both the weak points of his adversary as well as moments that are without danger for himself. Because every attack passes through this preparatory phase of its trajectory (a sort of void) before the point where it reaches real effectiveness, even when more than one attack follows another in a seemingly uninterrupted sequence, there always exist during the course of an attack some instants of vulnerability (or of void) that are something like flows and ebbs.

After the very short instant in which an attack is effective, there comes a relatively longer moment during which the fist or the foot is being withdrawn. This is a potential moment of attack for the adversary. Unleashing a fresh attack makes it possible to cover up this weak point, but never completely. So there is always a moment of vulnerability after an attack.

The tactics of distance must relate to the moments of vulnerability, or void, and to the moments of real danger.

With regard to the attack with the arm or leg extended in kime while moving the body forward, the instant of vulnerability (the time it takes to turn the arm or leg into a weapon) is relatively shorter than for an attack from long range in which the body does not move forward. Because once the arm or leg is extended, as long as it can stay in the state of kime, it functions like a stick held at an angle perpendicular to the body being moved through space by a movement of the body from the rear forward.

Taking the Initiative in Setting Distance: The Interaction between the Range Limits of the Two Opponents

As far as the distance in combat is concerned, in the second stage, the first thing that must be done is to become aware of the range limit of the opponent in relation to one's own.

When the range limit of the opponent is greater than our own, we must not cross this boundary except at the moment of vulnerability that occurs before and after the opponent's attack or at the moment of void that can appear in both the opponent's posture and his mental state at certain moments in the combat (this will be our subject matter in chapter 4).

When the opponent's range limit is smaller than our own, we should maintain the initiative in setting distance and begin our attack before the opponent comes close enough to bring us within his range limit. We should attempt to keep the combat within that narrow zone situated beyond the opponent's range limit but inside our own. We must be extremely vigilant during the moment of vulnerability that comes during the preparatory phase of our attack (which must be focused on a precise point) and maintain a mental tension that will make it possible for us to react to a possible attack by the opponent.

In these two situations, we must prevent the opponent from

gaining the initiative in setting the distance. In a combat on the second level, holding the initiative in setting the distance is the first point of contention. Hand or foot attacks at this point are ploys in the battle to dominate the control of distance.

The ability to sense range limits must be interiorized to such an extent that we feel crossing the boundary of our range limit or that of our opponent the same way we might feel entering or exiting a magnetic field.

When the range limit of an opponent is more or less the same as our own, the principal effort will tend to become anticipating moment by moment what attack our opponent is preparing, controlling his potential range, and taking the initiative ourselves in determining the range of attack. And in combat, whatever the opponent is like, once we have crossed the boundary of his range limit, we are in the "magnetic field" of attack, and we must, on the one hand, detect the moments of vulnerability in the opponent (thus far we have only defined two modalities of them, those movements preceding and following an attack); and on the other hand, we must maintain our defense in our own moments of vulnerability.

If we consider karate goshin-do as a way of self-defense, then ensuring our own safety is primary. The idea of safeguarding oneself provides the orientation for training. That is why blocking techniques take on major importance; the techniques of attack have their place within the perspective of defense.

When setting the distance in combat, blocking techniques ensure safety from the opponent's attacks, and in addition, they provoke moments of vulnerability in the opponent if he launches dangerous attacks.

In karate combat, the primary role of blocking is not mere parrying; it goes beyond that. In fact, when one executes a real block, it marks the beginning of a counterattack. If properly done, the block nullifies the opponent's attack for a span of time that might be very short, but is long enough for a counterattack. Therefore, before and after executing a block, our posture must be one of perfect balance so that we will be able to react immediately. We can block an opponent's attack in its preparatory phase as well as in the moment that it takes on cutting force.

When fighting an opponent whose range is longer than ours, we must pass through a zone in which the opponent can attack us but he is still out of our range. Two factors can provide us with safety when moving through this zone: our ability to perceive a moment of void in the opponent's state of mind and our ability to block.

As an old Chinese proverb says, "You can't catch a baby tiger without entering its den." A practitioner who is sure of his block is capable of crossing the boundary of the opponent's range limit, and when the opponent attacks, he can put himself in a position to take the initiative.

The progression from block to counterattack can be described in terms of cadence:

First Stage: *dum-dum-dum*. The first *dum* is the opponent's attack; the second is the block; and the third is the counterattack. This rhythm is the most rudimentary one for defense and counterattack. It is difficult to overcome the adversary using this, since defense and attack each constitute independent and separate moments, but it is with this that the learning process must begin.

Second Stage: *dum-duhdum*. The first *dum* is the attack; the *duhdum* that follows expresses the block and counterattack brought together, but the cadences of the attacker and the defender are separate: the counterattack happens immediately after the block, with the block taking place at the end of the opponent's attack.

Third Stage: *duh-dum*. *Duh* is the opponent's incomplete attack and *dum* is a counterattack. The counterattack takes place at the vulnerable point in the first attack (during the preparatory part of its trajectory). This is what is called in Japanese *sen-te* or *deai*, meaning the "technique that precedes." To accomplish this, one must seize the instant when the opponent's attack has not yet taken explicit form and is still just in his mind.

Fourth Stage: *dum*. The counterattack reaches the opponent before his attack gets beyond his mind. His intent to attack has not yet been concretized. Thus it appears from the outside that just one combatant has attacked and won, but this is the result of anticipating the opponent's attack and from the ability to react precisely during the opponent's moment of vulnerability.

Fifth Stage: Cadence of nothing. At this stage combat disappears, and it could be said that this is the ideal of combat. But to avoid any mystification, I would say that the cadence of nothing goes beyond the framework of the martial arts, that it is the sought-after goal that is never attained. Some people interpret the cadence of nothing as the cadence that allows one to foresee the combat and thus to step out of its way so that the combat never takes place.

These five stages correspond to levels of ability attained by combatants that enable them to impose on a combat, surely and without fail, the rhythms I have described. This does not mean that only combatants who have attained such and such a level of advancement will always perform in the course of a combat in accordance with the corresponding rhythm. For example, the counterattack that I summarize under the simple rhythm *dum* can occur in a combat between opponents who have not reached what I describe as the fourth stage, but in that case it will happen by chance. Real progress does not take place unless the technique in question is mastered with definite certainty. A rhythm achieved by chance is not considered something that has been truly acquired; it remains a goal that must still be pursued.

3. Maai as a Temporal Interval during which Awareness Lags behind Physical Movement

An older master, more than sixty years old, in diminished physical condition, often possesses less technical dynamism and less physical force and resistance than his young second-stage students who are twenty to thirty years old. But in combat, his superiority in the two other dimensions more than compensates for this handicap.[3] From the point of view of the maai of space, his maximal reach is often less than that of his young students, but he is their superior in his ability to sense the distance between his opponent and himself and to perceive the moments at which his opponent's awareness becomes separated from his movements.

Our awareness does not follow the rapid movement of our gestures in a homogeneous fashion. For example, when we attack a certain spot on our opponent's body, at this precise instant our awareness is focused on the point we are going to strike, which therefore means that it is polarized, and it is that state of awareness that makes the blow to that spot happen. As we have seen above, an attack carried out with kime takes effect at the last instant, the instant at which the hand or the foot becomes integrated with this highly polarized awareness. In the course of an attack, even though such moments always last only a very short time, we can still notice a moment in our mental and physical movements where our awareness becomes a little detached from the preparatory action of the attack. Our awareness does not adhere with the same intensity at every moment to the movement made by our hand or foot. During the preparatory trajectory, our awareness is much less dense than at the moment when it starts to become polarized.

We can observe this kind of temporal gap in our awareness, not only during a movement of attack but also in the course of various other movements. Such gaps are determined both by our level of physical force and by how concentrated our mental state is. These gaps can occur, for example, while blocking, dodging, displacing the whole body in order to attack or defend, feinting, and so on.

It is this temporal gap in our awareness in the course of combat that I call the temporal maai. This is an interval during which a lag exists between our awareness and our physical movement. It could be said that as a consequence of such a gap we present a kind of void to our opponent.

This instant of unequal density of awareness and movement is extremely short from the point of view of our ordinary, daily-life sense of time. But it is relatively long in terms of the cadence of combat in karate goshin-do.

A very advanced level in perceiving the maai temporal will make it possible for an older master to sense that an attack is being prepared by his opponent and to grasp the moment when the opponent projects on him the conscious concentration that precedes his attack, coming just before the onset of his movement.

THE NOTION OF HYOSHI

Miyamoto Musashi wrote in his work *Go Rin No Sho* (Writings on the Five Elements, or best known as *The Book of Five Rings*):

> Hyoshi is found in all things, but in the art of the sword, it is impossible to acquire it without training. . . . In the art of the sword, hyoshi exists in several forms. It is very important to learn about concordant hyoshi and then about discordant hyoshi. And it is important among the great and small, and slow and fast hyoshis, to distinguish concordant hyoshi, the hyoshi of ma [interval of distance], and discordant hyoshi. This last is essential; if it is missing, your sword will not be sure. In combat, knowing the hyoshi of the adversary, I must utilize a hyoshi that does not even occur to him, and I will be victorious by bringing forth the hyoshi of emptiness from the hyoshi of wisdom.

When we observe the distance between two combatants in its temporal development, we perceive changes in that distance—sometimes small, sometimes great—and we can discern a certain rhythm in those changes.

During combat, we have a cadence for each movement—whether it is dodging, blocking, or attacking—and for us this cadence represents a constraint, just as the cadences of our adversary do. No movement is separable from certain rhythms, both physical and mental. Even when we are apparently immobile, our muscles are contracting and relaxing and we are breathing, so we do have a rhythm connected to the movements we are making and are going to make.

In combat, we live each moment amid waves of rhythm or cadence. The subjective time of the combatant does not flow in a smooth or uniform manner.

The Japanese notion of hyoshi refers, in the example above, to rhythmic spatio-temporal intervals produced by the reciprocal relationship between the two combatants, and at the same time to the cadence of each one of them, which is closely related to each one's breathing and mental state.

I would like to propose the following as a definition of hyoshi on a general level, not confined to the martial arts: "Hyoshi is an integrated set of cadences that brings together as rhythmic elements several human subjects and their surroundings within the framework of an arranged cultural activity. This integration of cadences results in a balance or an overall harmony."

1. The Notion of Hyoshi in Japanese Culture

The importance of hyoshi in many cultural domains, such as tea ceremony and Noh theater, has often been pointed out. For example, Inazo Nitobe writes,

The art of drinking tea . . . is a poem that draws its rhythm from harmonious movements.[4]

In the tea ceremony, both the person preparing the tea and the person drinking it pass the time of the ceremony within an arranged space, performing certain movements that are blended with a mental state of harmony. The subjectivity of the participants moves in time and space. For someone watching from the outside, the result of their activity is the harmonious and rhythmic movements of the tea ceremony. The water is heated, the tea is prepared, and the participants drink. But in order for the tea really to be drunk properly, the participants' movements, their mental state, even their way of existing in a given space must harmonize perfectly with the space, with the time, with nature itself. In this way, it can be said that, with regard to the tea ceremony, a rhythm, or a cadence, is created.

This rhythm is interpersonal. There is the relationship between the person who prepares the tea and the person for whom the tea is prepared, and also the relationship of these two to the others in attendance, with all of whom a reciprocal rhythm is established.

Moreover—and this aspect must be underlined—this rhythm is established through working with objects and in relationship to the entire environment. In Japanese culture, it is precisely through entering into a relationship with objects that a cadence or rhythm is established, and it is this cadence that allows us to enter into harmony with other human beings or with nature.

Thus the Japanese apprehend objects without dissociating them from the rhythm of the gestures they make in relation to these objects. The same goes for their fashion of relating with other people. The manner in which they apprehend abstract or concrete objects is much more indefinite than that of Westerners, who consider objects in themselves, defined by characteristics that can be objectively described.

We must view this as a profound attitudinal difference with regard to nature. In the Japanese tradition, nature was never an object of study, but was considered as a much vaster subject that contained man himself.

Even describing the relationships among all the parts of the tea ceremony as we have just done corresponds more closely to the Western way of looking at things. It talks about harmony among the ceremony's diverse elements, namely, the preparer, the drinker, those in attendance, such and such particular objects, the chosen location, and beyond that, the environment as a whole, that is to say, nature.

But for the Japanese, it is the overall, global situation that is determinative. Here, each person, rather than regarding himself as a subject over against others, tends to efface himself as an ego in order to permit the harmony of the whole to emerge. In this situation, each person expects to be able to sense the universe, or—to express this in a Western fashion—to enter into a unity with the universe in which the ego is not experienced as such. This harmony, which can be said to be experienced passively, is made accessible by respectfully following a very precise cultural formula, which always includes a series of specific movements unfolding in time.

Zeami, a director of Noh theater during the Muromachi period, wrote in one of his works on the Noh play *Shi Ka Do* that within the content of Noh there exists skin, flesh, and bone.[5] In more precise terms, the skin is the fact of the spectators' perceiving the technical forms of the play, the flesh is the execution of these techniques, and the bone is the depth of heart from which the performance arises.

Another way of looking at this is from the viewpoint of the appreciation of Noh theater. From this point of view, "skin Noh" is Noh theater that is pleasant and can be appreciated by neophytes as well as by connoisseurs. "Flesh Noh" is not very pleasant initially, and neophytes will not be able to appreciate it, but to a cultivated audience it is seen as a very natural, successful expression of the art and as profoundly admirable. Finally, in the case of "bone Noh," there is not even time to appreciate or admire any single element because everyone is so totally absorbed that there is no possibility of distinguishing the dramatic techniques from the emotions one feels.

Thus the highest level of Noh theater consists not only in the actors' capacity for expression but in the harmony created by the union of the actors and the spectators, a union that includes the music and the space in which the performance occurs.

The actor's manifestation is not unilateral. No actor can achieve bone Noh without entering into harmony with his surroundings. Noh does not allow for egocentrism in the actor. The actor must not concentrate on himself. Despite the fact that his role might be the principal subject of the performance, he must not have an awareness of being the focal point; rather he must have a sense of being part of the whole, which includes the actors, the spectators, the music, the place, and the time. The way in which the space/time of the theater is experienced is more centrifugal than centripetal.

By contrast, the Western ego, being more centered on itself, tends to collide with other egos in the external world. They are objects to be studied, to be conquered, to be fought with, to come to agreements with, to arrive at reconciliations with. The phenomena of identification are thus highly accentuated. Similarly, in contemporary theater, alienation tends to be a key element, which additionally places the spectator in a critical position.

The Japanese ego, on the other hand, being more open and centrifugal, constantly seeks to enter into union with its surroundings. As we have just seen, in Noh theater as described by Zeami, a union can be reached between actor and spectator as a result of the cultivation of a diffusion of ego into the totality. Hyoshi, which is the rhythm of this union, the cadence for entering into this harmony with others, is a manifestation of this way of being.

Formulating this in a Western fashion, we may distinguish the following factors in Noh theater: the main actor, the secondary actors, the musicians, the spectators, the set, and the setting of the theater, which might be a natural one. All of these factors must enter into harmony. From the point of view of the actor, to enter into harmony with all the other factors means to move within an overall pattern of cadences (manifested as the hyoshi), to be in harmony with everything and not regard oneself as a subject who is acting.

In the consciousness of the actor, there exist several cadences for harmonizing his gestures with the other theatrical elements (actors, music, etc.), with the spectators, and with the surroundings. The "bone" actor (one who is said to possess "flower") perfectly realizes an overall unity that integrates all these cadences, that is to say, the hyoshi, which is nevertheless conditional upon a reciprocity that implies an analogous availability on the part of all the rest of the participants. The actor's ego is oriented toward an awareness of balance, of harmony with the whole. It is not he who determines the relationship with the others; rather he opens himself to a totality. Thus his orientation is quite different from that of a Western actor, who on the basis of an individualistic conception of the ego, acts, thinks, reflects, and observes the others and so finds his strategy as an actor.

Thus in Japan, a harmony created by the integration of the cadences of several subjects is what characterizes the traditional arts. Moreover an integration of this type is a major element in the deep structure of human relationships.

2. The Importance of the Practice of Hyoshi in Combat

Hyoshi in karate goshin-do has two aspects: one relating to oneself and one relating to the adversary. A combatant is subject to the internal rhythms of his body: all his movements and even his apparently immobile positions depend on the rhythms of his body and his mental state. In karate goshin-do, even when a combatant is making movements that appear very rapid and complex, they are never produced by chance. They are based on a system of codified movements, the breadth of range of which varies according to the kareteka. On the basis of this system, the karateka can even discover new movements. The codification of techniques in its repetitive aspect and the sequencing of techniques are dependent on establishing cadences of movement regulated by the physical sensations of the kareteka.

The onset of movements (attacks, blocks, dodges, etc.) is triggered simultaneously by the breath and by the ebb and flow of muscular tension. Relating properly to these makes it possible to execute movements that are both rapid and strong and also, I would even say, explosive.

Rhythm or cadence provides the combatant with a means of enlarging the range of techniques he has at his disposal. This is because they permit him to mentally integrate the series of codified movements whose active execution he has memorized to the point where they have become automatic.

The interiorization and mental representation of rhythm are so important that karatekas who have attained a certain level can work out new techniques based on mental images of rhythmic aspects of the body in motion. When we execute a movement, it constitutes a whole, and often in training, this movement is repeated in just one way. It seems to me necessary that to train in the most effective manner, we must distinguish three aspects—form, force, and cadence; and if we want to work on one or another of these aspects, we can vary the way we practice a movement so as to work on just that particular aspect, even though from the outside the movement may appear to remain the same.

For example, when we are trying to learn to bring a series of movements together into a sequence, we should not work on the force aspect, but rather on flexibility. In that way we can really assimilate the cadence of the movements to the point where it becomes automatic—of course always with the understanding that the form of the movements must be perfectly executed. During other phases of the learning process, it is necessary to bring in the force element. Often in karate training, force and cadence are not distinguished; but in my view the two are not learned through the same process, and our teaching method must take this into account.

The interaction between two combatants brings into play the whole range of cadences of each one of them, cadences related to movements, facial expressions, breathing, the ebb and flow of muscular tension, mental state, and so on.

The karateka enters into a cadence relationship with his opponent. He must find his own hyoshi by apprehending that of his opponent. He finds the rhythmic void in his opponent by relying on the harmony established between himself and the opponent. When the hyoshis of the two opponents are in close accord, the movements of the two complement and avoid each other. Such a rapport can remain in place even when the combatants don't move. Where such a rapport is present, it is difficult if not impossible to execute an effective and certain attack; in these circumstances if an attack does succeed, it does so only by chance.

Yagyu Munenori wrote in his work *Setsunintu* (The Sword That Kills),[6]

> Concordant hyoshi is bad, discordant hyoshi is good. When the hyoshis are in accord, it is easier for the adversary to use his sword, and when they are not in accord, the adversary cannot use it.

This expression is very subjective. Objectively, we might think that the consequences would be the same for both combatants when the hyoshis are in accord and when they are not. Munenori is trying to say that it is necessary to take the initiative by throwing the hyoshis into discord, by creating a discordant situation where you are active at the expense of your adversary. When the hyoshis of two combatants are not in accord, the one who is passive in this rhythmic situation cannot dominate, nor can he find with certainty a moment of attack. But the combatant who can take the initiative is certain to find a moment of vulnerability in the position and pace of the adversary.

One of the conditions for "striking after having won" is taking the offensive initiative by creating a discord in the harmony between yourself and your adversary in such a way that the cadence of his body is no longer in accord with yours. This creates a constraint that will momentarily impede his movements. To create this discord, you will have modified your hyoshi (your cadences) but your adversary will still be left adjusting his cadences to the previous phase. Thus you are aware of your hyoshi and of your opponent's hyoshi at the same time, whereas your opponent is off balance, since suddenly he can no longer find your hyoshi. When the combatants are on a high level, the confrontation between their hyoshis precedes the exchange of attacks and blocks.

Traditional training methods bring about progress in the dimension of hyoshi, without, however, seeking this result per se. The reason for this is that the notion of hyoshi has not been singled out. In my opinion, we can make more rapid progress by having the principal goal of our exercises clearly in mind. Thus, I would retain those elements in the traditional training methods that are helpful for making progress in hyoshi.

First, learning the katas correctly helps with the development of hyoshi in relation to ourselves. Second, certain forms of conventional combat enable us to make advances in hyoshi in relation to an opponent.

TRAINING METHODS

1. Katas

Literal translations of the word *kata* are "form," "mold," "type," and so on. Katas provide structure to a number of Japanese disciplines that have in common seeking to follow the do. Thus I would propose the following general definition of the term *kata*: "a sequence composed of formalized and codified movements underpinned by a state of mind directed toward the realization of the do."

Sequences corresponding to this definition can be observed not only in martial arts such as kendo, judo, or karate-do, where they are in fact called katas, but also in other traditional arts such as kado (flower arrangement), sado (tea ceremony), shodo (calligraphy), and also in classical Japanese theater and dance. In all of these disciplines, a definite effort is made to execute the katas with perfect form, to synchronize techniques of formalized movements with a particular psychological orientation. In practicing and perfecting the katas, the body, like a boat following a predetermined course, moves toward the fusion of physical movement with mind through which the sought-after perfection comes about.

In traditional karate, around forty original katas are known, to which can be added a number of variants. Most of these katas contain between twenty and sixty movements.

Katas have for a long time played a fundamental role in the communication of techniques of combat. In fact, all the classical techniques of karate-do are contained in katas.

A kata is always a codified transposition of real combat with several adversaries. Beginning with an initial situation, different each time, sequences of attack or defense are built up in response to supposed moves by the adversaries.

As we know them, katas are not the creation of a single master, but are condensed from the accumulated experience of a number of generations. This accumulated experience is what the katas transmit to us. We know their form perfectly, but their meaning often remains uncertain. There are several reasons for this. We train only in the kata, an exercise that is focused on executing a sequence. Even though each movement in the sequence is definite, without an adversary present, the situation to which it is a response is not obvious. It is a deliberate part of the traditional teaching of the katas that the action of would-be opponents is not explicit. Discovery of the significance of the katas' movements is meant to come as a function of a student's progress.

In addition to this, these techniques have sometimes been transmitted with a care to disguise them from rivals or from an oppressive power. This being the case, we can only suppose that certain parts of the code have been intentionally distorted so that the knowledge it contains will only come through to students who have received instructions concerning these alterations. Nonetheless, these movements have continued to be transmitted from earlier times, though most of the explanations for them have been lost.

Thus at the present time, no certain and sure interpretation of the katas exists, and those adepts who reach a certain level interpret them in the light of their attainments. This is one of the reasons for the diversity of karate styles we now encounter.

Within the framework of karate goshin-do, to begin with, we have to look for the meaning of each of the movements starting from its most apparent sense. After that, we must make an effort to rediscover the implicit meanings of the movements through the light shed on them by our personal practice as well as by a larger view. Let us take the following example. A parrying movement of the arm executed with a closed fist has a block as its most obvious purpose, but it may also be seen to have a grasping or throwing function if we consider that the closed fingers are closing around the wrist of the virtual opponent (since the kata is done by oneself). Thus it is essential to be extremely vigilant: each movement must be thought through on its own, but also in relation to the unfolding of the entire sequence of which it is a part. It is only through an overall vision that a deeper interpretation of a movement can come about.

In the old way of teaching, a single kata, worked on for years by a master and his disciples, condensed and concretized a whole set of technical and strategic accomplishments. Thus each karateka worked in depth on a small number of katas in which his entire attainment was embodied.

In former times (and I have gathered accounts from both contemporary older masters and also various written works), a master who had himself learned in this manner would work on a kata with certain students of his, selected according to their level of accomplishment, practicing this kata with variants that might apply to the form of the movement or to the strategy of its use in combat. It was the totality of this work that constituted the meaning of the kata. Each of the movements composing this kata had several variants, the significance of which could touch upon the very fundamentals of combat. Thus the kata transmitted from master to disciple served to some extent as a mnemonic device. But during the recent period, in which the practice of karate has been propagated on such a vast scale, in most cases, this sort of transmission has disappeared. Even in the past, it was only possible with highly accomplished students. The meaning of katas continues to be transmitted, but only in fragments.

At the present time we are familiar with a certain number of katas whose forms are relatively fixed, but they are no more than nice empty forms if the content of them eludes us. Today, we cannot hope to rediscover the somewhat occluded content of a kata by shutting ourselves up in a single style. Each style transmits to us in a fragmentary manner this or that aspect of a given kata. Thus we must aim at going beyond particular styles and at the same time devote ourselves to systematic exploration of what each style can yield. But—and this is an essential point—going beyond a given style can only take place at an advanced stage of development, and to reach this level, one has to have passed through study of the forms of this given style.

In this regard, the Japanese formula of *shu ha ri* precisely defines the method that must be followed in learning an art. *Shu* means "to respect," "to follow the model or the ideal form." This explains why it is necessary to begin by learning a kata perfectly. *Ha* means "to liberate oneself from the effort of learning in order to go beyond the first stage, while continuing to hold to the path that has been indicated." Effort here is more personal, but continues to strive toward the perfection of a style. *Ri* means "to move beyond the form." At this level, the kata as form disappears. Effectiveness is realized as a function of the circumstances. It is only at this third stage that going beyond styles can be genuine. But from the beginning, while respecting the practice of a given form, the mind must not shut itself up in it as though it were the absolute reference point.

Such an approach might seem contradictory while on the first level—to devote all of one's energy to realizing, in the tiniest details, a form that one is going to abandon later on. But taking a longer view, this detour into details we are going to leave behind does not appear futile, because this work must also be complemented by both intuitive and historical reflection on the earlier stages of the transmission of katas. For example, now we practice karate on a smooth wooden floor, but earlier the ground was stony and irregular. Certain foot movements include within them, along with whatever other purpose they may have, seeking better balance on uneven ground. Formerly, combat sometimes took place by moonlight or lantern light; therefore it was necessary to take the best possible position with regard to the light source. Thus in practicing certain katas attentively, we encounter certain tactical intentions that were incorporated into them by the old masters.

Finally, studying ancient documents, especially those of masters of the sword, as I have begun to do here, will help us to grasp the significance and strategies of combat. Study of the other martial arts (aikido, jujutsu, kendo, etc.) is indispensable—we need only recall that during the feudal period, warriors did not practice only a single martial art in isolation but several at the same time.

It should be added that during development in hyoshi in relation to oneself, the kata provides us with an excellent exercise for assimilating the cadences of combat. Since katas are the codification of a combat, they allow us to experience the cadences that pervade combat from beginning to end, which is not the same thing as learning a simple sequence of movements. Several cadences follow each other in each kata; they constitute the overall harmony that is unique to that kata. These cadences guide us in finding the way the movements are linked with one another.

Through correct daily practice of katas, we can expand our ability to synchronize cadences.

2. Conventional Combat

Conventional combat is always practiced with control. Attacks must be halted at a distance of three centimeters (1.18 inches) all the way down to zero centimeters from the opponent, but they must be carried out with kime. The two combatants take turns working on attack and defense. There are three typical forms of conventional combat:

A simple attack-and-parry chosen in advance from among the basic techniques, repeated three or five times (san bon kumite *or* go hon kumite). Here the practitioner learns the concordance of cadences, which is the most elementary level, the starting point for hyoshi. He works on the cadence through repetition. He also learns to better evaluate the maai (distance and time interval) on the basis of the most simple form—maintaining one's distance.

An attack chosen in advance with an unspecified parry-and-counterattack, executed just once and based on a much broader range of techniques. These techniques are to be carried out in their purest form (*kihon ippon kumite*). The two essential moments are the attack and the counterattack, with a block or dodging maneuver taking place in between them in order to create the conditions for an immediate counterattack. More precisely, in this exercise the block or the dodge are not important in themselves but have as their purpose to create a vulnerable moment in the opponent during which the counterattack can take place.

In this form, hyoshi is improved by exercising with a much more varied range of techniques that are not entirely predictable. This is the beginning of learning the discordances. Here the practitioner can develop the ability to sense the difference between concordance and discordance in the cadences.

In the course of this form of training, as in the previous one, the combatants do not cross the boundary of their limited striking range. They maintain a safe distance, but with a very small margin.

An attack with parry and counterattack. The first attack may be determined in advance or left unspecified. The block or dodge and the counterattack are not specified (*jyu ippon kumite*). The combatants cross the safety boundary, but they are obliged to control their attacks and maintain vigilance in avoiding the opponent's counterattack (deai). They work at a very high level of tension, endeavoring in this way to approximate a real combat situation. When the adversary attacks with determination and a very high level of tension, it is very difficult to react without having a level of tension equal to his. And the ability to be effective in executing the various techniques of combat also requires a corresponding level of psychological tension. If the level of tension of the two opponents is the same, then the technique plays the determining role. In jyu ippon kumite, the practitioner works on mobilizing tension as well as on the ability to relax mentally.

The practice of hyoshi takes place in this situation of tension, and the practitioner learns to adjust and disrupt the harmony of his own cadences and those of the adversary in various situations.

His efforts must be oriented toward mastering the disruption of hyoshi.

Through conventional combat, we can gain practice in the dimension of maai and hyoshi in relation to an adversary at the same time as we gain practice in mastering the techniques. The most important things are to develop precision in the movements, in the perception of distance, and sensitivity with regard to the concordance and discordance of hyoshi.

3. Free Combat

In traditional free combat, the combatants control their attacks, but freely.[7] Some conventions must still be maintained, because this is not real combat. To work properly in free combat, one must first perfect control, precision in movement, and perception of the opponent's attacks. Each of the combatants must be capable of recognizing the validity of controlled blows, that is, each must be able not only to control his own attacks but to recognize the potential effectiveness of the controlled strikes of his adversary (sufficiency or inadequacy of force, etc.).

In free combat, our aim is to integrate the maai and the hyoshi while moving through the full range of techniques, but at the same time, remaining within the conventions. Traditional free combat is only possible if both combatants have reached a high enough level of accomplishment.

Nowadays, traditional free combat as it has been adapted for sports competition is practiced by karatekas whose levels of accomplishment are not always up to this type of exercise. For this reason, for one thing, accidents occur; and in addition, there is resentment on the part of combatants who are often not capable of recognizing the potential effectiveness of blows struck by their opponents, or their own for that matter. Sometimes bouts continue without being stopped by the referee or the combatant who has in fact been defeated, even though a valid but controlled blow has been struck. Often the referees themselves are not capable of discerning which controlled blows are effective ones.

This is one of the reasons behind the current tendency toward forms of uncontrolled combat, with or without protection, and toward a system of determining wins by points scored or by knockout. This tendency is obviously completely contrary to the objectives of karate understood as a form of budo: "Don't win after having struck, but strike after having won." This budo approach would exclude blows struck by chance and would tend toward acknowledging the absolute effectiveness of blows struck without control. Another problem with the new tendency is that it displaces the principal objective of budo, which now becomes victory in combat rather than the development of the karateka's abilities.

Maai and hyoshi permit a combatant to approach absolute victory, partly by enabling him to detect the void moments in his adversary and partly by allowing him to assess and keep track of distance and thus be aware of moments of safety and danger.

In bare-handed combat, we are safe as long as the hand or the foot of an adversary does not touch us, even if he misses by only a millimeter. The same is true in sword combat.

It should be clear that all combats unfold in time and space through the application of physical techniques that are governed by specific cadences, and these are integrated into the awareness of each of the opponents in connection with his own movements and at the same time into the awareness of both the opponents in connection with their reciprocal relationship.

That is why accurate and rigorous assessment of spatial and temporal distance as well as the assimilation and mastery of the various cadences are extremely important and must be the objective we work toward through our method of training. In other words, the objective of development in karate goshin-do should be evolution of the awareness that makes it possible for us to exist more intensely in time and in the movements of combat.

Nevertheless, in order to attain the very high point of development we are seeking, we have to pass through another door, the door that opens into the larger and more elusive realm of yomi.

5

THE DIMENSION OF YOMI

YOMI HAS BEEN CALLED "the art of intuitively sensing and foreseeing [the moves of] the adversary." The dimensions of maai and hyoshi remain inseparable from that of yomi to the extent that intuitively sensing one's opponent is part of maai and hyoshi, but in this latter case, as we have seen, this is limited to a very definite field. Time, or temporality, is the meeting point between the two dimensions.

The dimension of yomi is not a closed one (see diagram, p. 60), because it extends into areas that are more mystical and religious than they are rational, notably into the realm of metaphysical mental states sought after by some religions.

Here I will deal with this dimension only to the extent that it is tangible, using my readings and my personal experience as a guide. I will confine myself to the presumption concerning the dimension of yomi in the Japanese martial arts that there exists a vast realm, which is very difficult to demonstrate, but which nevertheless is not purely the creature of some mystical interpretation.

When the dimension of yomi is seen in terms of the role it plays in the martial arts, it becomes, on the whole, clearer and easier to grasp. The image of the indomitable old master ceases to be a myth and presents itself before our eyes in a concrete fashion. At the same time, we discover a physical and psychological state that is available to everybody through gradual stages, even though historically, in the cultural tradition of Japan, this ultimate stage of budo could only be attained by following an obscure path that could not be delineated in words.

Westerners have happily taken up this image of something ineffable and enshrouded it in mysticism, rather than making it an object of study. But gaining an understanding of the dimension of yomi, as well as that of maai and hyoshi, does not at all require of us that we attain mastery of them on the level of practice. We can gain a basic understanding, which will then simply provide us with guidance toward practicing these dimensions on a higher level.

As an art of intuition and foresight, yomi is one of the means of communication utilized in Japanese life. It goes beyond language, gestures, mime.

The word *yomi* is usually translated "reading." More precisely, yomi is an inflected form of the verb *yomi*, "to read," which also at the same time means "to decipher." And indeed in traditional Japanese culture, one is expected to "read" between the lines or read the blank margins of the page. It is comparable to "reading" the face of a person who is silent to discover a thought that has not been expressed in words; in such a case we must intuitively sense an implicit intention, which might even be the opposite of what has been said in words. The expression *i shin den shin*, "from mind to mind," which comes to us from Zen, is now used in the popular language to mean nonverbal communication. In Japanese, the act of "reading" (yomi) is not limited to decoding a concrete expression, but also includes the art of intuiting and anticipating ideas, thoughts, feelings, intentions, and desires.

Yomi is not only oriented toward concrete and visible objects but also toward their environment, even if this is seemingly nonexistent and does not contain any visible, tangible things.

Before beginning our study of yomi in the martial arts, I would like to raise a question. Are we capable of sensing another person's intent to attack by means of a sixth sense or by using our five senses heightened beyond the usual level?

Leaving this question open, I will first examine the concrete conditions in which the practice of yomi arose, and then I will analyze this practice from the point of view of two elements: (1) temporality, and (2) the ability to sense an intent to attack directed against us.

YOMI IN THE WARRIOR CULTURE

Let me begin by sketching the historical and cultural context in which the dimension of yomi developed in the traditional martial arts. This dimension is a cultural product of the order of warriors, whose culture was formed through a process of introspection. The importance introspection acquired was a result of the warriors' way of life.

Eight centuries passed in the history of Japan between the appearance and disappearance of the order of warriors. The order of warriors arose in the middle of the eleventh century. The first government dominated by the warriors, the shogunate, was formed in 1192 and continued until the fifteenth century. At the end of the fifteenth century, a war among the feudal lords began that lasted until the end of the sixteenth century. In 1603, a central power was established by the shogun Tokugawa that imposed peace on the feudal lords. The ensuing period was called the Tokugawa period, which lasted until 1868. At the beginning of this period, in 1639, the shogun Iemitsu decreed that all relations between Japan and foreign countries be cut off. Contemporary Japanese culture, the culture of today, began with an apparent break with the culture of the Tokugawa period,[1] but this older culture continued to exist below the surface. During the Tokugawa period Japanese society was closed in on itself. This closed society was highly structured, an institutionalized feudal system divided it into four hierarchical orders. At the top were the warriors, then came the peasants, then the craftsmen, and finally the merchants. In addition there was a group that was considered to be "nonhuman."[2]

Beginning in the fourteenth century, the Japanese began to develop relations with the external world beyond the ancient zone of communication with China and Korea, going as far as Vietnam and Burma. At the beginning of the sixteenth century, the Portuguese Jesuits and then the Spanish arrived in Japan and introduced, along with their religion, the Western culture of science and technology. These began to have a major influence in Japan. Until the end of the sixteenth century, Japan remained open, and not only the merchants but also the warriors were attracted by the world outside, especially by the knowledge coming from the West.

I would like to emphasize that by this time Japan had developed a culture of its own and had accumulated a certain amount of what might be called "cultural capital." We might speculate that, if the policy of openness had continued and the energy of a part of the population had continued to be directed toward the outside world, Japanese society would not have turned in on itself to the extent that it did, and thus the role of introspection in the culture would have been less. But in fact, an introverted condition on the scale of Japanese society as a whole characterizes the culture of the period after the closure of the country. The determination with which the closure was maintained is typical of the approach to life the Japanese warriors developed. Thus the closure of Japan must be considered not only a historical fact but also a determinative force in the formation of a culture. With the order of warriors being shut in on itself during a long period of peace and social stability, interiorization and introspection became a major factor, which put its stamp on the culture as a whole.

To illustrate the rigidity of the policy of the shogunate, let us look at the example of weapons. The end of the preceding period had been marked by numerous wars among the feudal lords. With the introduction of rifles by the Portuguese in 1543, Japanese production of these weapons developed with extraordinary rapidity.

In fourteen years, three hundred thousand arquebuses were manufactured in Japan. But during the ensuing Tokugawa era, manufacture of firearms abruptly slowed, and no evolution in the technology of firearms took place. The rifles manufactured in Japan at the end of this period were, with very minor differences, the same as those manufactured at the beginning of it. Similarly, a transformation of the military tactics of the feudal lords had begun toward the end of the warring period when firearms were introduced, but this transformation was halted by the new social order, which was based on a stable hierarchy reinforced by the central power's policy of bureaucratization of the warrior order.

At the beginning of the warring period, the sword was seen as a noble tool of combat. Each warrior used several swords in the course of a battle. The practical and utilitarian aspect was prioritized; the form of swords was solid and heavy in keeping with a concern for effectiveness. By contrast, during the Tokugawa period, the sword ceased to be a mere material object and came to be regarded as the soul of the warrior. It became the symbol of the dominant order. Its form was refined. The curvature of the blade and the shape of its point underwent change. Although there were no wars among the feudal lords, the practice of the martial arts evolved because of the extremely intense daily combat exercises to which the warriors devoted themselves as the key mark of their order. The practice of training face-to-face with an opponent led to refinement of the movements, and a great part of the energies of the warriors was invested in ongoing perfection of this activity. The techniques and tactics of sword combat were painstakingly studied and modified over the course of long years. At the same time certain movements and techniques were codified into katas. These were considered to be perfectly finished forms, and performance of them gradually took on a ceremonial appearance. Warriors directed their efforts toward perfecting each technique and each movement, and a high level of execution of all the details became essential. Value was placed not only on defeating an adversary, but also on the manner of obtaining the victory.

"Don't win after having struck, but strike after having won." During the regime of the shoguns, the order of warriors were the functionaries of the apparatus of state, which was hereditarily and hierarchically organized. The highest values of the warriors were loyalty to their lord and honor. Tourneys and duels were frequent affairs. Willingness to face death was an integral part of the social image of the warrior. I would express this by saying that among the Japanese warriors, the time of death was running ahead of itself.

It seems to me necessary here to point out that temporality is not identical in all cultures, but varies from one to another. I am not talking about cosmic time considered as independent of human existence, but about the human perception of time, the experience of living in time, people viewing and conceptualizing their lives in time. In this sense, the time in which people express themselves and understand the world around them is cultural.

The temporality of the Japanese warriors is explained by their way of life, whose historical development we have briefly sketched. The attitude of the warriors toward death is the most meaningful example of this.

"The thought of death is the first thing a *bushi* must have in his mind, day and night, from the January-first holiday until the thirty-first of December." That is the first sentence of the *Budo Sho Shin Shu*.[3]

> Obliged to make the choice between death and life, the bushi should choose death without hesitation. This will always lead us toward the best.
>
> —HAGAKURE

The number of such citations we could draw from the bushido writings of the Tokugawa period is great. They show that the bushi is supposed to live in relation to death. That is to say, the warrior should see the phenomena of the external world and act toward them with a sense of his death, which is the measure of his life. In examining the manner in which these warriors lived or were supposed to live, it seems to me that the notion of death was constantly present throughout life. In this sense, among the warriors, the time of death ran ahead of itself.

In the contemporary period, we rediscover the attitude toward death of the ancient Japanese warriors in the kamikazes of the Second World War. From the moment they made their decision to participate as kamikazes, these young men lived the time of their death well in advance of their actual death. This is what makes their conduct at once quite unique and quite dramatic.

The Japanese term is more precisely *kamikaze tokko tai*, meaning "special kamikaze attack team." It referred to the combatants who went to attack American ships in planes without landing gear and without fuel for the return flight, the plane itself being the bomb.

The word *kamikaze* means "the wind" (*kaze*) "of the gods" (*kami*) and evoked the memory of the typhoon winds that twice drove off the fleet of the Huns when they were threatening to invade Japan (in 1274 and 1281). At that time, these were the only attempts at invasion Japan had faced. This action of the winds was integrated into a nationalist ideology that was revived at the time the groups of the kamikaze tokko tai were being formed. At that point, that ideology seemed to be saying that Japan is the land of the gods, the gods have already protected it in the past, and the sacrifice of the young tokko tai will save the country. This nationalist ideology, which is based on Shintoism, had already served to unify the country around the emperor-god, and later on it would help to justify the political expansionism of Japan.

From the moment a youth entered the kamikaze tokko tai, he accepted his death, from which he was, from then on, separated only by a brief time. His entire life was henceforth directed toward death, and he applied himself toward eliminating all his desires to the contrary. The letters the lads of the kamikaze tokko tai wrote to their families show the inner struggle they were going through in order to reach this point. In these letters, they often tried to console their parents and to justify their death by finding reasons for it. Thus they stifled their desire to live, and, well before their death, their entire mental approach was directed toward it. They interiorized the time that lay before them by linking it to their death, which was already inevitably planned for and expected to take place when they were in their prime, in the full strength of their youth. This was not to be a peaceful death, a passive one, but a death in action, literally an explosive one. Their moment of renouncing life was thus not to be at all like a candle being plunged in water, but rather like a firework going off. Their mentality was not that of a man awaiting execution. It was a mentality that was focused on the moment at which their existence would explode, and it demanded of them that they direct themselves toward that moment with the attitude that society expected of them. That is, they were expected to die like Japanese warriors, like kamikazes. They were expected to enter into a kata-like mold[4] that would explode in a few hours.

Their situation was institutionally and technically set up to prevent any other outcome than death. They departed on their journey without any possibility of return. Thus we could say that, in both individual and social terms, the time of their death was running ahead of itself. This contrasts with Western forms of heroism in which everything possible is done to ensure a safe return for the participants once the mission is accomplished.

The case of the kamikazes is a unique one, restricted to a particular moment of history, but it clearly shows a tendency that I believe to be characteristic of the warrior culture of Japan. The time lived in the moment of combat is situated on another plane; it is the dimension of one instant in relation to the time of a lifetime, but its nature must be understood in the context of the overall view of that lifetime.

TEMPORALITY IN THE DIMENSION OF YOMI

Through what I understand by the notion of temporality in combat, especially in the dimension of yomi, we can better understand the state of awareness that has been sought after in the martial arts and has also often been realized in the religious practice of Zen. It is certainly no accident that, starting from a certain level, adepts of the way of the sword have often turned to Zen in order to attain a faultless integration of mind and body.

In the temporality of combat, what counts is the density with which time is lived. The combatant wins not only through physical force, through the techniques, through the maai and the hyoshi, but also through the depth, intensity, and fullness of time experienced during the combat. The combat may last a few seconds or a few minutes, but what counts is not the external measure of time. Every second passes for everybody, and we can objectify that with a chronometer, but time in combat is subjective time, and it could be said that we fight also through the quality of our time, because the quality of time is a determining factor in combat. We must understand that this subjective time is not always identically filled by our existence, which is more or less intense moment by moment.

We see our adversary for a second, two seconds, or ten seconds, but this does not mean that we see him the whole time. There are moments when we do not see him, even if we continue to look at him.

An attack launched by a highly accomplished combatant can happen at a moment when he is being watched by his adversary, yet without the latter seeing it coming. This does not necessarily entail tremendous speed. There is a tendency among sports practitioners of karate to evaluate the level of an opponent on the basis of the speed and flexibility of his movements. This means seeing things in terms of just one dimension and failing to recognize the quality of subjective temporality, which is much more decisive.

In the reciprocity of time between adversaries, time is an alternation of the presence and absence of awareness. Combat techniques are therefore based on the ability to sense absence of awareness on the part of the adversary, and to keep one's own time as present as possible in the movements of combat.

In order to bring out this notion of temporality, let us look at the examples of some early masters of the sword. Even though these masters did not focus on temporality as such, we can see in them mental techniques that make it possible to reach and maintain a particular state of mind. As I see it, temporality is an underlying factor in these techniques. Seeing this permits us to make an analysis that unifies them.

The sayings of Ito Ittosai, a sword master of the sixteenth century, were collected by his disciples:

> The most important thing in combat is the ma [distance]. When our mind is attached to the ma, we cannot react completely freely, diversifying our moves. When we are detached from the ma, the ma is necessarily accurate.

Ittosai is not talking about a training procedure. What he is describing here is the ideal state, that is, the personal state that training aims at. And indeed, Ittosai himself attained this level. In his time, it was normal not to speak of stages but only of final results.

In the course of the earlier stages of development, a constant effort has to be made to discern the ma, to coordinate our perceptions and our movements with the distance between ourselves and the opponent. Here Ittosai is talking to adepts who have this stage behind them. The act of consciously trying to discern the ma causes the mind to enter into a time that is attached to an object. According to Ittosai, the only way one can unfailingly discern the right distance is by becoming able to do it unconsciously, that is, by placing oneself in expanded time. I will make clear what I mean by "expanded time" by analyzing Miyamoto Musashi's text "Concerning State of Mind in the Art of the Sword" from the *Go Rin No Sho*:

> One's state of mind during combat need not be different from one's ordinary state of mind. In daily life as well as in combat, one must keep one's mind open and straight, neither

too tight nor too loose, nor off center. One must place one's mind in the center and move it gently, even at moments when one is off balance. One must train well in all that. When the body is calm, the mind does not stop, and when the body is moving quite violently, the mind remains calm. The mind must not be carried away by the body nor the body by the mind.... In the art of the sword ... it is necessary to distinguish between looking and seeing.... One must look at what is distant as though it were close and at what is close as though it were distant.... It is important to look at both sides without moving one's eyes.... In the art of the sword, there are five guard positions: the high position (*jodan*), the middle position (*chudan*), the low position (*gedan*), the right-side position, and the left-side position. All these positions have the purpose of cutting down the adversary, and from the moment one takes up one's sword, it is in order to cut down the adversary.

To strike the adversary, there is a way of striking with a simple cadence. It consists in striking at the distance that is both within my range and my adversary's, without moving either my body or my mind, at the moment when the mind of my adversary is hesitating between several techniques.

When both my adversary and I are ready to attack, the body is in attack position and the mind is concentrated for the strike. Then my hand moves naturally; it accelerates and strikes with force. It is a blow without thought, unconscious. At a distance at which the adversary's sword and my own barely touch, I strike extremely hard without even slightly raising my sword. This is the *sekka* (stone and spark) strike.

After having thus followed the real way of the sword, face-to-face with my adversary, I perceive what he is thinking before he begins his move. When he means to strike, I stop him at the letter *s*; when he means to close, I stop him at *c*; when he means to jump, I stop him at *j*; when he means to slash, I stop him at *s*. This is what I call "grabbing the pillow."[5] But one must not try to do this all the time. I make all my movements spontaneously, following the Way. . . .

When I do not see the mind of the adversary, I make his shadow move; . . . then his mind will be reflected by his sword. In the way of the sword, through the habit acquired through combat, one arrives at being able to discern the movements of one's adversaries to the point of being able to perceive everything—particularly the distance and speed of their swords. And at the time of combat, it is on the mind of one's adversary that one places one's attention.

Miyamoto Musashi always lived alone. He conceived of his life in its totality as a quest for perfection in the way of the sword. His daily life, even in its tiniest details—his personal grooming, for example—were integrated into this quest. He expressed his combat experiences in images. Thus he wrote that it is necessary to keep one's mind at one's center, at the center of everything, that the movement of the mind must never stop. When he writes that one must not decentralize one's mind, he means that one must not attach it to anything with partiality.

This image translates what he experiences in the time of combat that permits him to have his body react before any conscious reflection takes place. It describes a state of mind that allows him to react appropriately to each situation of combat, everything else being left outside the field of awareness. This is what is sometimes expressed in training by the saying "Relate to the mind as though sleeping." This mental approach causes us to move in a time that is not flowing by in linear fashion but rather expands into the whole universe. The idea is to put oneself into expanded time, or in other words, to perceive all aspects of the situation at once on the same level. Everyday time is experienced in a manner more or less analogous to the image of speech unfolding one word after the other. But expanded time opens us to a multiplicity of perceptions simultaneously; it clearly contrasts with the hierararchization of perceptions implied by speech unfolding in a perpetual process of classification. This latter operates by making the field of consciousness narrower and more definite; whereas the time of combat is time during which verbalization (even directed toward oneself) loses its privileged place. Images concerning combat time are elaborated after the fact in an attempt to communicate to other people who have also experienced this opening of awareness to the realm of simultaneity.

"Keep your mind in the center"; in this state of mind, the habit pattern acquired during previous combat maintains a direction that underlies consciousness and guides our bodily movements. Definite fixation on an object or an aspect of the situation disrupts the expanse of this openness and causes our mind to fall back into linearly channeled everyday time. But in the mental state of expanded time, neither the body nor the mind triggers our movements by itself. Rather both come together in perfect agreement in our movements, whether they are violent or calm, whether they are movements of attack, dodging, or blocking. This is how our movements occur when they are directed by the orientation of mind evoked by the images Musashi uses.

When he writes, "In combat we must distinguish between looking and seeing," Musashi is expressing that in combat, distances must be apprehended not by intellectualizing them but by feeling them sensually, even on our skin, through the intermediary of the eyes. We look with our eyes, and this vision is not experienced as a perception of a spatial interval, but like a direct contact coming through to us through the thickness of space. We cannot get to this kind of sensitivity to distance except by entering expanded time. When we do that, it is possible to "see what is far away as being close and what is close as being far away"; and "to look at both sides without moving your eyes."

I don't see any point in commenting further on this essay by Musashi on the techniques of combat, because the techniques are only concretizations of the state of awareness (expanded time) we have just analyzed.

Yagyu Munenori writes in his *Heiho Kaden Sho*,

When one rests one's mind, the mind goes away somewhere and often stays where it has gone.[6] To avoid this, a beginner, when he strikes with his sword, should withdraw his mind from his hand so that it does not remain there when the blow has landed. A combatant of a higher level of accomplishment will let his mind go freely, but it will not remain wherever it arrives. Thus his mind is not like a dog pulled by a leash. . . .

In the art of the sword, our mind is variable according to changes in the adversary. When the adversary raises his sword, our mind goes to the sword; when he moves to the right or the left, our mind follows him. This variability is un-predictable and leaves no track. Since the mind does not stop anywhere, it dissolves like the white line of the wave behind a boat that is moving away. . . .

It is important to train oneself in not fixating one's mind— not on the movements of the adversary nor on one's own movements, even though they may make slashing or stabbing movements.[7]

The Zen monk Takuan (1573–1645) writes,

I am asked in what part of the body should one put one's mind. I reply: If you put it in your right hand, your mind will be taken by your right hand; if you put it on your eyes, it will be taken by your eyes; if you put it on your right foot, it will be taken by your right foot. No matter what part you put your mind on, it will be absent from the rest.

So where should you put your mind?

No place. If you put it no place, it fully and thoroughly expands throughout your body. When you need your hand, it makes your hand function. . . . You use the mind just where it is, according to the movements of your opponent. . . . The true mind is like water, and the mind lacking in confidence that is fixated on one spot is like ice. Ice and water are essentially the same thing, but you can't wash yourself with ice. To do that, you have to melt it and make it flow in the desired direction.

Therefore it is necessary to melt frozen mind so that the water that then flows covers the entire body. That is what is called true mind.

If the mind is fixated on an object, when you hear, you do not really hear; when you see, you do not really see. This is because there is an object in the mind. If you succeed in annihilating this object, the mind will become the mind of nothingness, which will function appropriately for everything.[8]

Thus Yagyu Munenori and Takuan write that to keep the mind stable, it must not fixate on any other thing, but be unceasingly mobile. When you fixate your awareness on something, you enter into objectification, and from there into your habitual way of evaluating time. By entering into a kind of total oblivion of the external world, you allow your mind to move freely. You are detached from the temporality that is attached to objects; you let your awareness become unbound by the movement of time.

Dream is another example of deviation from the everyday perception of time. Between the moment when the alarm clock sounds and the moment when the sleeper wakes, or during the brief instant of falling if one falls out of bed, dreams can occur that seem to last a long time. Thus a very brief stimulus can occasion a dream, which may or may not take the form of a story, but during which, in the course of a duration that is subjectively very long, a multitude of images arise. Similarly, the example is often cited of people in an automobile accident who, during a short span of time in which they are moving through space, feel that they have mentally relived their whole lives. What we are dealing with here is a sudden emergence of the unconscious, which explodes the perception of time, expanding it onto another level. I would put forward the hypothesis that in the expanded perception of time that occurs in combat, as in the expanded time of Zen, the absence of fixation on an object helps to bring about an opening of the field of consciousness. In that opening, what would normally be the object of conscious (centralized) perception is perceived as being on the same level as all the other parts of the field of consciousness that are normally relegated to the unconscious level. It could be said that the dialogues between advanced practitioners of Zen that have been written down are mostly incomprehensible, but in my opinion, that is because the verbalizations that have been recorded are only a part of their exchange. Their exchange is not limited to the conscious verbal field of the speakers, but extends beyond that to all the manifestations and sensory perceptions of the unconscious, and these also come into play in the dialogue.

The notion of expanded time permits us to better understand how to establish this relationship with the unconscious. Zen will continue to seem incomprehensible if we reduce those dialogues, which for their participants were situated in expanded time, to conversations situated in everyday time. Through their spiritual work, the Zen monks had arrived at a state of nothingness within time, and it is through communication of that state that Zen greatly helped certain adepts of the art of the sword.

Historically, the notion that the art of the sword and Zen form a unity appeared in the seventeenth century. In that period it became a leading idea and gave rise to such discussions as "Should a Zen monk become an adept of the art of the sword?" Discussions of this sort did not occur without producing a certain amount of mystification. In the *Tengu Gei Jutsu Ron* (Questions to a God on the Art of the Sword), Niwa Jurozaemon (1619–1741; also known as Issai Chozanshi), a sword master, situated the way of the sword in relation to Zen:

I asked, "Is the Buddhist who is detached from both life and death capable of developing mastery in the use of the sword?"

The god replied, "The goal is different in Zen and in the art of the sword. The Zen monk becomes detached from life and death by placing himself from the beginning in the same state of mind as one who is dead in order to find eternal peace in the cycle of life and death. Thus it is possible that if he were surrounded by enemies, even if he were torn to pieces, his mind would not move. But this training would not help him at all to safeguard his life; simply put, he is not afraid of death. . . . A beginner in the art of the sword, if he does not train, absolutely cannot discover the spirit of the sword, even if he receives a lesson from a very great Zen monk."

In my view, if it is true that Zen and the art of swordsmanship come together, it is in the realm of their relationship to time. The Zen monk, in his religious quest, arrives at an expansion of time. But for him to fight effectively, this expanded time would have to be channeled through skill in combat that can only be created by long years of training. A person who has had enough Zen practice can arrive at expanded time, but he will lack the necessary ability in combat.

The psychological state of nothingness that Zen points to can do no more than make it possible to become detached from time, to move freely in time. Another example will provide a further illustration of the relationship between Zen and swordsmanship.

Yamaoka Tesshu, who lived from the end of the feudal period into the beginning of the Meiji period, is considered one of the greatest masters of the sword of his time. From the time of his youth he was very talented and very accomplished in the art of swordsmanship; but in 1863, at the age of twenty-seven, he met another sword adept, Asari Matashichiro, fought with him, and was entirely dominated by him. Tesshu was deeply marked by this encounter and began to critically examine his inadequacies as a practitioner of swordsmanship. He said to himself, "If I can't defeat him, my sword is dead; I must surpass him." He felt that his defeat had not merely been a physical one but had occurred due to his lack of spiritual development. Day and night, for ten years, he devoted himself both to training with the sword and to Zen practice. At the end of ten years, when he met Matashichiro, he still felt the sensation that in his adversary's presence his body as well as his mind were diminished. After this experience, the image of Matashichiro continued to be in his mind night and day. For seven more years he devoted himself to training in the sword and in Zen. In 1881, at the age of forty-five, the image of Matashichiro that had haunted his nights and days disappeared following a kind of Zen enlightenment experience. So he went to ask Matashichiro to fight him. First Matashichiro made him fight one of his disciples. At the very outset, the disciple cried out, "I have lost before even fighting!" After this, Yamaoka Tesshu fought with Matashichiro, and after a short time, Matashichiro lowered his sword and said, "Finally you have attained the essence of the art of the sword."

On another occasion, Yamaoka Tesshu, seeing a kata executed by Master Yamada, who was seventy years old, expressed his admiration by saying, "So something as profound as that exists in kendo. It is not absolutely necessary to practice Zen as long as one can base one's training on this kata." It is true that adepts of the sword have often had recourse to Zen, but it was not the totality of Zen that they were seeking but rather something that the art of the sword and Zen have in common.

SAKKI: SENSING THE INTENT TO ATTACK

"To read" in the sense of yomi, that is, to sense the opponent intuitively and know his moves in advance, is only possible on the basis of a particular state of mind: expanded time. This has nothing to do with analyzing the psyche of the opponent. In sensing him, analysis and reflection are inapplicable, except outside of combat. During combat, reasoning should not appear, except briefly. Otherwise our mind will fixate for a longer or shorter time on the object of the reflection or the analysis—his posture, his position, the movements of his foot or fist, his feints. If we are to perceive these things, it must be without fixating our mind on any one particular point.

The Zen monk Takuan, who in his text applies the Buddhist precept according to which "all desires are born of the mind's attachment," writes,

> In meeting the attack of the adversary's sword, if you look at his sword, your mind will be fixated on it and you will not be able to react appropriately. You will be killed. When you see the sword coming, don't stop your mind on it, don't even think of striking by harmonizing yourself with the hyoshi of the adversary's sword. Don't reflect, don't reason, but as soon as you see the sword in front of you, just grab it, reaching as far as the opponent's hands. If you place your mind on that of your adversary, your mind will taken by his; and if you place it on your body, it will be taken by your body, so you must not place your mind on your body either.

Reflection requires a moment of stopping on the object of reflection. That is why we must read the adversary without passing through a process of reflection. The state of awareness in which one does not fixate one's mind on anything, which we have explained in terms of expanded time, is the most important of techniques and the one that is most difficult to learn. Through that state of awareness, according to the martial arts tradition, one becomes capable of sensing one's opponent intuitively, that is to say, of foreseeing an attack without even seeing the opponent, of foreseeing the path of the blows he is going to deliver by anticipating the movement of his mind.

Without getting into a mystical explanation of this, in order to provide a further idea of this conceptually elusive area, I will simply offer the following examples. They have nothing in them that would surprise a contemporary Japanese, because in traditional Japanese popular culture, the kind of ability they illustrate, though it is very difficult to express in concrete terms, is a familiar one.

One day, Yagyu Munenori was admiring cherry blossoms in a garden. Nearby was his servant, carrying his sword. The servant looked at him and thought, "Even though my lord is a great master of the sword, if I attack him from behind while he is contemplating the cherry blossoms, he will not be able to defend himself." Suddenly, Munenori looked in the four directions, then went into the house and sat down, leaning against a post. He stayed there for hours without moving. The servants became uneasy and began to wonder if he had gone mad. Finally one of them dared to ask, "A while ago, your mood changed. Is there something bothering you?" Munenori replied, "I am thinking about something I do not understand very well. After years of training, when enemies attack me, I can sense their intent to kill me [sakki] before beginning to fight. A little while ago, as I was looking at the cherry trees, I felt sakki. I looked around me, but there was nobody but my servant, not even a dog. I didn't find anybody who might be my enemy. I thought it must be the result of a deficiency in my development on the way that I felt that." Then the servant who had carried the sword came and begged his pardon. "In fact, a while ago, while looking at you, I had the thought that at that moment I might be able to kill you with that sword." At that, Munenori was content. "Good. Now I understand."

This sort of story is very widespread in Japanese literature, in which many tales are told of the budo adepts of yore who were able to sense sakki (intent to kill on the part of their adversaries). In particular, there are stories about sword masters who were attacked at night, often from behind, and were able to defend themselves without seeing their adversaries by relying on this sensation.

The example of Master Ueshiba, the founder of aikido, is particularly interesting, because it involves an adept of budo living in contemporary society. His son, recounting the life of his father, cites these words of his:

An instant before my opponent attacked, I saw a small white light, the size of a pea, moving from one place to another. Immediately afterward, the bokken [wooden sword] followed exactly the same path as this light. Thus I could easily dodge the sword by dodging this white light.

Master Ueshiba said that this white light was the sensation he felt of the intent of his opponent directed against him.

Similarly, in karate, during the years following the War, some adepts continued to live with their wartime mind-set, and trained using attacks that were very close to real combat. Master Kubota, one of the disciples of Master Funakoshi, told me that he had been attacked several times from behind by his students, who were looking for some way to defeat him. He said he felt their intent to attack. Once, he was attacked from behind with a punch as he was walking through a doorway. He blocked the blow and his opponent was thrown against a wall two or three yards farther into the room. He gave me this example in order to show that a block must at the same time be a means of overcoming the adversary.

One of the essential conditions for becoming able to sense the intent to attack without looking at the adversary is accumulation of combat training and practice. But in addition it is necessary to maintain an ongoing state of readiness to react against any attack. This is only practically possible in a social context of the type we have just described, where the intent to kill may be manifested in a direct physical confrontation.

In Japanese society, the ability to sense other people through intuition has played and still plays a very important role in everyday life. The current expression *hara gei* (literally, "the art or technique of the gut") means sensing each other intuitively without anyone explicitly expressing his thoughts.

This expression comes from the archaic idea that thought resides in the belly. Let me give you a personal example. Having a gut sense that one of my French friends wanted to have a get-together with our friends, I organized such an occasion, thinking for sure that he would then pitch in to help me with the event. I figured it was my role to initiate things, and it seemed a matter of course for me that he would then help me, since he was the one who wanted the get-together to happen in the first place, even though he hadn't said anything to me about it. That was a Japanese way of behaving on my part. However, the expected help from him never came. When I talked this over with my friend, he said, "I never asked you to do anything." At the time, that was a big shock for me, but for a Frenchman, it was quite a natural response. He had wanted the party to happen, but since he didn't have time to arrange it, he hadn't asked me to do anything about it either. Then, when it did happen, he acted as though something nice had come about by chance. For a Japanese, this desire of my friend was as clear as an explicit request that he might not have been able to make without feeling awkward about it. It is completely natural for Japanese people to anticipate in this way what others implicitly desire.

This is a form of communication that does not occur through the medium of speech, or at least speech does not express the message directly. Often even in the highly modern Japanese business world, interpersonal relations are carried on through such nonexplicit signals in accordance with this traditional model.[9]

Thus the art of sensing one another intuitively is very deeply rooted in Japanese culture, and it is on this basis that yomi developed.

We have given an account of how the psychological state of openness and availability we have called "expanded time" makes it possible to interpret the instructions given by masters of the sword for attaining the highest level of development in that art. Placing oneself in expanded time is, in my opinion, an essential condition for practicing yomi in combat and for sensing the intent to attack on the part of one's adversary. I would like to stress here that this is not something unique to the way of the martial arts but rather a very intense application of a proclivity that is very widespread in Japanese culture. Not only art but also to a certain extent traditional Japanese craftsmanship seem to me to depend on this kind of intensified awareness.

Calligraphers, for example, meditate for a long time, but they do not calculate their lines. Once a stroke is made, it is done. A calligrapher must try to seize the psychological moment in which the entire figure to be executed is integrally present in his mind. At that point, the calligraphy is done all at once; once the calligraphy has begun, there is no stopping until the end. It is inconceivable that one would pause to calculate. In my opinion, concentration is necessary here in order to enter into expanded time. One sees the blank page not only consciously but also through the unconscious. In this ultimate state, it could be said that the calligrapher has the sensation that it is not he himself who makes the line, and this is precisely because he has entered into expanded time.

The process of making crafts takes much longer, but there are still decisive moments in the execution of the work. For example, the craftsman who makes a sword has time to reflect and calculate while he is beating the blade, but the moment he dips the hot blade in water or the moment when he finishes its line demand tremendous concentration. The craftsman must seize the moment in which he is at one with the object he is making. As noted in chapter 3, this is referred to as kiai. We have already encountered one sense of this word—the shout. However, in the present context, kiai divides into *ki*, the "energy that fills the universe and is the essence of everything," and *ai*, which means "meeting." The resultant sense is of apprehending in one's gut the moment of deep harmony with ki. Here this is done through the intermediary of the object one is making.

Clearly, then, apprenticeship in this sort of artisanal work does not take place through the medium of texts or treatises by means of which one might make objective studies of the technology involved, but through long years of practice.

The master craftsman communicates his knowledge stage by stage, without explicit explanations, calling upon the intuition of the apprentice. The craftsman senses the kiai without calculating it. This is the reason there are no good written works objectifying these artisanal techniques. This is one of the reasons, I think, that traditional Japanese technology did not develop in the direction of scientific knowledge. Fundamentally, the attitude toward the object produced is different from the attitude of Westerners. The object is fabricated on the basis of a kind of intuition that does not leave behind it any reference points of the sort that would be left behind, for example, by a calculation. Rather the moment of making is one that is enclosed within itself. The learning experience that comes about remains with the maker and thus cannot be transmitted; it cannot serve as a basis for a later elaboration. Finding a method of communicating yomi that would make it possible to transmit the inner knowledge accumulated in this nonobjectified manner in a number of different disciplines is interesting in many ways and is worthy of becoming—in fact, must become—the subject of multidisciplinary study, study for which this book attempts to set forth the initial premises.

I do not pretend to have completely explained the dimension of yomi, which touches upon the most profound aspects of Japanese tradition and is situated on the borderline between psychology and parapsychology. I nevertheless think I may have shed light on the two aspects of Japanese culture that serve as the foundation for this dimension and permit us to grasp its significance. These two aspects are the ability to sense another person intuitively and the experience of expanded time.

FIVE SWORD MASTERS OF THE TOKUGAWA PERIOD

THE INTERPRETATION of the structure of budo I have just given can, I think, serve as a key for a better understanding of the works of the Japanese budo masters.

In this chapter I will present the works of five sword masters of the Tokugawa period. Budo, as we know it today, reached its high point in the course of the period of feudal peace that preceded the opening of Japan to the modern world. Chronologically, at first the bow was the most important weapon of the Japanese warriors. At the time of the appearance of the warrior class, the word for "warrior" meant "archer." The practice of warriors changed when they became the leading group in Japanese society. During the Tokugawa period, real wars ceased to occur, and archery became mainly an art. The way of life of the warriors was formalized. Each warrior had to learn eighteen martial arts. The sword became the daily weapon of Japanese warriors. Warriors were never separated from their swords, even keeping them within reach while they were sleeping. The sword became the symbol of the warrior. This is why it is the works of the sword masters of this time that mark the formative moments in the development of budo. Karate, as I see it, must be based on budo as illustrated in those works in order to attain its full potential.

It is not really possible to accurately render the meaning of the Japanese texts of this period by a literal translation into Western languages. The reason for this is that in the culture of this period, written works were never intended to completely transmit a given content. Rather, their role was only to provide a basis for intuitive comprehension. In comparison with Western languages, the words of Japanese texts convey a less definite content; the content is broader, more image-oriented and symbolic than the concepts conveyed by words in Western languages. Moreover, relationships between ideas are not as clearly expressed in grammatical structure in the Japanese writings as they are in Western languages.

I have tried to transpose into English the meaning of the original texts that follow as clearly as possible; however, I have not attempted to be explicit where that might have diminished the richness of the author's ideas. I have chosen authors whose influence continued on in Japan until the modern period.

YAGYU MUNENORI

Yagyu Munenori was the sword master to the family of the shogun and as a result acquired considerable political power.[1] He had great political and cultural influence over the third shogun, Iemitsu (shogun from 1623 to 1651). His office was then transmitted to his descendants, which gave them the rank of feudal lords.

In the course of his development in the way of the sword, he was strongly influenced by Zen Buddhism. His relationship with the Zen master Takuan is clearly evident in his work. Zen interested Munenori primarily as a spiritual technique. He also performed in Noh theater, which he associated with his practice of the sword. The story is told that during the performance of a Noh play at the palace of the shogun, Munenori was deeply impressed by the fact that the actor Kanze Sakon was giving an absolutely flawless performance. This caused Munenori to view the actor's performance in the spirit of actual combat with the sword. At one point, Munenori experienced an extremely brief gap in the actor's portrayal of his role and called out, "Kiai," in a low voice. After the performance the shogun asked Munenori why he had cried, "Kiai." First Munenori congratulated Kanze, who then said,

I am sorry to have presented an imperfect expression of my art. I performed to the best of my ability, but at one moment, there was an unexpected change in the decor, and at that point my Noh was disturbed for a very brief instant.

That was the moment at which Munenori had cried out.

This anecdote illustrates the way the different arts converge when one has sufficiently perfected any one of them.

I will cite Munenori's best-known book, *Heiho Kaden Sho*, once again:

When you train sufficiently in all areas, you arrive at the point where you move your hands, feet, and body without moving your mind, and without even thinking of your training you are spontaneously able to coordinate the result. At this stage, you yourself don't even know where your mind is, and even the demons cannot divine the movements of your mind. The whole training is devised to lead you to this stage. The most important thing is to train in all areas to forget this training. And by forgetting everything, you act very aptly without any thought or reflection.

Tactics have a first level and a second level. The real tactic is the one that the adversary recognizes as a tactic but which he can't grasp nor, as a result, parry. When I use a tactic, if the adversary gets caught up in it, I win by making him get caught up in it. And if seeing that, he does not get caught up in it, I use another tactic right away. In that case, I defeat the adversary who did not get caught up in my first tactic.

When a superficial fault acts as a stepping-stone to the truth, this fault becomes the truth. We find this in the teaching of Buddhism.

The next passage refers to the state of ken and *tai*. *Ken* means "to engage" or "to start off"; *tai* means "to wait."

From the outset, concentrating, you prepare harsh attacks and try to strike before your adversary does—this approach is called ken. You wait without immediately attacking your adversary, who intends to strike first—this approach is called tai. It contains a heightened sense of caution. In combat, it is essential to distinguish between ken and tai. There are very important relationships of ken and tai between the body and the sword. You move your body closer to the adversary adopting the state of ken, but you keep your sword in a state of tai. And by provoking the adversary with your body, your feet, and your hands, you make him attack first, then you defeat him. Thus to bring on the adversary's attack, your body and feet keep the state of ken, and your sword the state of tai.

Relationships of ken and tai also exist between the body and the mind. You keep the mind in a state of tai and the body in a state of ken, because in a state of ken, the mind tends to get carried away too violently. That is why you keep your mind in a state of tai and the body in an active state of ken. In this way, you can induce the adversary to strike first and thus defeat him. When the mind is in ken, you tend to want to kill your adversary, which will make you lose. But it is also sometimes recommended to keep the mind in a state of ken, and the body in a state of tai, which means to let the mind stay active without letting up and keep the sword in a state of waiting.

Through this technique, you win by making the adversary attack.

The characteristic of the Yagyu family school is to overcome the adversary by letting him attack first. Munenori writes from this point of view in another work of his, entitled *Gyoku Sei Shu*:

> Among the innumerable variety of techniques, there are not really so many fundamental ones. They are as follows:
>
> 1. Defeat an opponent who does not attack by provoking his attack and defeating him at the moment he attacks.
> 2. Defeat the adversary at the moment he attacks.
> 3. Against an adversary who knows the first tactic, feign a moment of void in yourself, and when he attacks, defeat him as he strikes.
>
> There are only these three.

"Striking unilaterally is not sure," Munenori writes. This means that a sure attack technique is launched by attacking at the moment in which one has perceived the vulnerability of the opponent and not simply by seizing the initiative of attack.

For Munenori, this vulnerable moment basically appears when the opponent attacks. Applying his approach to karate, I have come up with the following version of his three techniques:

1. Find the vulnerable moment in the opponent at the moment when he launches his attack. The kind of counterattack that is executed in the void instant when your opponent is just beginning to launch his attack is called "deai."
2. When your opponent does not attack, provoke his attack by feigning one of your own, or by changing your distance or your rhythm. In this way, you get your opponent to move and you defeat him by seizing the moment of void that appears at the very onset of his motion.
3. Pretend a moment of vulnerability in yourself, and when your opponent attacks, defeat him.

In the same perspective, in karate, the block and dodge are not considered just simple defenses, but as means of creating a vulnerable moment in the course of an opponent's attack.

When you are facing an adversary who is waiting for you to attack [tai], you try different tactics to try to get a glimpse of his reactions. You see as though you were not seeing; you don't fix your gaze anywhere and you perceive the adversary as a whole. . . . In Noh theater also there is a twofold gaze. With your gaze pointing in one direction, in reality you are looking in another. It is relatively easy to reach the adversary with your sword, but it is very difficult not to be reached at the same time. When the adversary attacks, trying to cut me down, I calmly let him attack, keeping track of the distance at which his sword will not reach me. The adversary attacks believing he will reach me, but he does not reach me, and at that point his sword is dead—I attack and I win. The attack launched by the adversary fails, my sword takes the initiative, and once I have struck, I do not stop my mind on this fact, because it will relax and the adversary's blow will land. . . . Once you have struck, without heeding whether or not your blow has been decisive, you must continue to attack—once, twice, three, four, or five times— until the adversary is unable to lift his head. Only with this spirit will the first blow be decisive.

I will only give here a part of Munenori's writings on hyoshi, since I have already cited his work in chapter 4:

When the adversary deploys his sword using a large hyoshi, I employ a small hyoshi, and when the adversary uses a small hyoshi, I employ a large hyoshi so as not to be in agreement with the hyoshi of the adversary. If the hyoshis agree, it is easier for the adversary to use his sword. In Noh theater, neither the music nor the dance can be performed if one does not know the whole of the chant. It is the same in the way of the sword. It is necessary to distinguish the movement of the adversary's sword from the movement of the adversary himself. That corresponds to grasping the whole of the chant. Once you have understood the sequence of the adversary's movements, you can easily react. Up to the very moment of exchange in combat, you must not relax your mind, thinking that your adversary is in a state of ken. And you must make the root of your mind firm.

"Hearing the voice of wind and water"—this means keeping your surface calm while the depth of your mind is active. In itself, the wind does not have a voice; it only has a voice when it touches something. Thus the wind blowing in the heights is silent, and when it blows lower, it makes sounds by touching the woods, the bamboo, all things. Then it becomes noisy and full of haste. Water also, when it is falling from above, has no voice; it acquires a voice when it touches objects below. Hearing the voice of wind and water means keeping your surface calm and your depths active, without letting up. It is not good to move the body, hands, or feet with haste. . . . "Hearing the voice of wind and water" corresponds to reason in nature. Moreover, when you attack violently on the surface, it is essential that your mind not be carried along with this violence. Thus surface movement will not trouble the mind.

When the surface and the depths are agitated, you are troubled. The spirit of ken ["engaging," "starting"] and the state of tai ["waiting"], understood as movement and calm, must be split up between the surface and the depths. The water bird appears calm even while it is moving ceaselessly with its feet. You must train in keeping your mind vigilant, in being like a water bird, who though calm in appearance moves its feet unceasingly. Then only will you arrive at coordination of your external movements and your state of mind.

Wanting only to win is a sickness. Only seeking to acquire technique through accumulated training is also a sickness. Always wanting to attack, or again, being set on waiting, is also a sickness. It is also a sickness to think of getting rid of these sicknesses. I understand by "sickness" a state of mind that is rigidly fixed. These various sicknesses reside in our minds. That is why we must control them mentally in order to free ourselves of them.

To overcome these sicknesses, Munenori proposes controlling them in two stages. Here is the first:

Thinking without thought, fixing the mind without fixation—this means that trying to get rid of these sicknesses of the mind is a thought. The sickness is a polarized thought. Thus we can get rid of our thought through a thought; when that thought disappears, we arrive at the state of nonthought. This means that you get rid of a thought through a thought. When the sickness of the mind is eliminated through thought, the thoughts that aim at eliminating thought are also eliminated. It is the same thing as doing away with one mold by means of another. . . . This means, there is a thought, but the thought does not exist. . . .[2]

There is a higher level of development where one can say that getting rid of the sickness means not having the thought of wanting to get rid of it, because it is also a sickness to want to get rid of the sickness. Therefore, without thinking at all, when the state of sickness appears, you leave it as it is and you remain in that state—and that is getting rid of the sickness. It is because there is a sickness in your thinking that you want to get rid of the sickness. As long as the sickness remains, this thought remains fixed in the mind. Thus you can never win. How should we understand that? I will respond as follows—this is why I have distinguished two successive stages.

First, during the first stage, you must train your mind as I have indicated. Then when you have reached the second stage, you succeed in getting rid of thoughts without trying not to fix the mind, because the sickness is a fixated thought. A monk asked his master, "What is the Way?" The master replied, "The Way is nothing but the everyday mind." . . . It is a state in which you get rid of all the sicknesses of the mind and the mind remains ordinary. Even if there are sicknesses, you do not get rid of them by putting your mind into a state of sickness. For example, when you shoot a bow, the thought of shooting the bow disturbs the shot; and when you use a sword, the thought of using the sword makes the sword swerve. When you are doing a calligraphy, the thought of doing a calligraphy limits your stroke. When you are playing music, the thought of playing music disturbs the music. . . . In all the ways, the true Way is not the way that is fixed in thought. Those who have attained the Way have nothing in their heart. . . . The mirror that is always clear has no form; that is why it reflects whatever is in front of it. It is the same with the thought of one who has accomplished the Way. The absolute emptiness of thought permits him to react to everything, and this is the ordinary mind. The true adepts are the ones who accomplish all things with this ordinary mind.

Before seeing with the eyes, you must see with the mind. This is fundamental. That is to say, you see first with the mind, then with the eyes, then with the body, the feet, and the hands.

THE REFLECTION OF THE MOON IN WATER

In using the tactics of combat you must know the distance at which the sword of the adversary cannot reach you. The reflection of the moon in water symbolizes the technique with which I establish this distance without my adversary perceiving my doing so. In combat, it is necessary to accomplish this situation of the moon in water. . . . When you look at the moon, it appears not to move; when you look at the water, it does not reflect the moon, but suddenly you perceive the reflection of the moon on the water of the pond.

Munenori is saying, in my opinion, that the establishment of distance must be made to happen in the same way as the reflection of the moon arrives on the water.

Here are the ideas that Munenori developed concerning muto (sword combat without a sword), a technique in which he achieved exceptional mastery:[3]

Muto does not necessarily mean wresting the sword away from the adversary at all costs, nor does it mean satisfying your own vanity by taking away the adversary's sword. This is a technique that enables you not to get cut in two by the adversary's sword when you are not carrying your sword. . . . It is not snatching away his sword when that is what he expects. It is also not snatching away the adversary's sword if he is preparing to prevent having it taken away, because someone who is trying to avoid having his sword taken away cannot slash someone, since his mind is attached to not having his sword taken away. For me, keeping myself safe is a triumph. The goal is not to snatch the sword. It is a technique for staying safe when I am not carrying a sword. The technique of muto does not aim exclusively at taking away the adversary's sword. It is a technique that permits you to use anything at all. If you are capable of taking away the adversary's sword when you don't have one, you should be able to use anything at all; for example, if somebody attacks you with a long sword, you should be able to defeat him with just a fan or a cane of bamboo. That is the basis of muto. The fundamental goal of training in muto is to perfect maai. You learn at what interval [temporal or spatial] the adversary's sword won't reach you. Thus when you know the maai [the distance] of safety, you need have no fear of a sword. And when you perceive the distance of danger, you react appropriately. The technique of muto is the one I use when I am within a dangerous distance [one at which the adversary can reach me]. . . .

To acquire the techniques of muto, it is necessary to be prepared to fight bare-handed against an armed adversary. A sword is long, a hand is short. You cannot use this technique unless you are capable of crossing into the range at which the adversary can cut you down.

So you ask yourself, "Am I capable of fighting bare-handed against the adversary's sword?" Fighting with your bare hands means that the adversary's sword must be past my body, and I must be below the adversary's wrist. Then I grab him by the wrist.

Munenori adds,

In muto combat, I evade the adversary's sword by maintaining a distance of thirty centimeters [just under a foot] from it to ensure my safety, but when the blade of his sword comes closer, safety is not absolutely guaranteed.

Munenori writes that to be able to react smoothly and appropriately, both mental and physical ability are necessary, based on technique that is correct to the smallest detail. He says that these two abilities are not separate and must constitute a unity. Thus when a person has great ability, his mind does not get attached to anything in particular but extends over his entire being, and he is able to react appropriately and with complete freedom, without explicitly heeding any rules or conventions. When you are under the gaze of such a person, if you neglect for even a single instant to draw your sword from its sheath, this delay in combat signifies defeat.

According to the doctrine of Buddhism, the mind varies in accordance with different situations, and this variation is unpredictable. This maxim is of very great importance for Zen and also for the way of the sword. I interpret this in connection with the way of the sword. In swordsmanship, the different situations correspond to the different actions of the adversary. My mind varies in accordance with each of my adversary's actions. For example, when my adversary raises his sword in order to cut me down, my mind goes to this sword; when the sword moves to the right, my mind goes to the right; when it moves to the left, my mind goes to the left. Which means that the mind varies according to the circumstances. What is important is the following: the manner in which it varies is unpredictable, which is to say that the mind does not stop; it dissolves completely like whitecaps or the white wake of a boat moving away. If the ever-varying mind were fixed, the result in combat would be catastrophic.

In order to present Munenori's thought through these texts, I have selected passages that in my opinion are applicable to the contemporary martial arts and that also best evoke his technique. Nevertheless, his book is not written in a scientific manner, and he often says that at some point he will show us the most important techniques, some of which were a family secret. For example, he ends the passage on the reflection of the moon in water by saying, "As far as distance is concerned, you must learn this directly." He uses this same formula to conclude a number of passages that are particularly difficult to interpret.

We have seen that Zen had a big influence on Munenori. He was the first sword master to affirm explicitly that the art of the sword and Zen are in some way the same thing. He made this affirmation after having attained a very high level of swordsmanship. Questions related to mental attitude came up for him, when having reached this high level of accomplishment in the art of the sword, he still found himself facing uncertainty. It was at this point that he turned to Zen. And it was on the basis of his study of Zen and his relationship with Master Takuan that he attained a state of certainty with regard to his art—that is, a state in which victory no longer had to reckon with chance.

Takuan's teachings to Munenori were recorded in the *Fudochi*. I give here the translation that D. T. Suzuki gives of one of the most important passages in this book:

> What is most important in the art of fencing is to acquire a certain mental attitude known as "immovable wisdom." This wisdom is intuitively acquired after a great deal of practical training. "Immovable" does not mean to be stiff and heavy and lifeless as a rock or a piece of wood. It means the highest degree of motility with a center that remains immovable. The mind then reaches the highest point of alacrity ready to direct its attention anywhere it is needed—to the left, to the right, to all the directions as required. When your attention is engaged and arrested by the striking sword of the enemy, you lose the first opportunity of making the next move by yourself. You tarry, you think, and while this deliberation goes on, your opponent is ready to strike you down. The thing is not to give him such a chance. You must follow the movement of the sword in the hands of the enemy, leaving your mind free to make its own counter-movement without your interfering deliberation. You move as the opponent moves, and it will result in his own defeat.

> This—what may be termed the "non-interfering" attitude of mind—constitutes the most vital element in the art of fencing as well as in Zen. If there is any room left even for the breadth of a hair between two actions, this is interruption. When the hands are clapped, the sound issues without a moment's deliberation. The sound does not wait and think before it issues. There is no mediacy here, one movement follows another without being interrupted by one's conscious mind. If you are troubled and cogitate what to do, seeing the opponent about to strike you down, you give him room, that is, a happy chance for his deadly blow. Let your defense follow the

attack without a moment's interruption, and there will be no two separate movements to be known as attack and defense. The immediateness of action on your part will inevitably end in the opponent's self-defeat. It is like a boat smoothly gliding down the rapids; in Zen, and in fencing as well, a mind of no-hesitation, no-interruption, no-mediacy, is highly valued.[4]

Yagyu Munenori had a very big influence on the samurai of the following period who practiced the sword in his school. During this period, the idea that the art of the sword and Zen are the same thing was widespread. As it was popularized, this idea was schematized. What remained of it in its popularized form was that ken equaled Zen, leaving out the whole process of learning and development that is really involved. Later on, we will cite the work of Niwa Jurozaemon (Issai Chozanshi), who, a century after Munenori, critiqued the approach of equating the art of the sword with Zen by clearly situating the two disciplines in relation to each other.

ITO ITTOSAI

Ito Ittosai was a great master of the sword who predated Munenori by a few years. Thus he developed his art at the end of the period of feudal wars and at the beginning of the Tokugawa period. Ittosai's school of swordsmanship was comparable in importance to that of Yagyu Munenori's, though it represented a separate current in the development of the art. We have very little precise knowledge concerning Ittosai's life. However, a number of anecdotes that have come down to us attest to the exceptional level he attained in the art of the sword. What follows is one of them.

Ito Ittosai paid a visit to a Shinto temple, where he spent seven days and seven nights in an effort to attain the ultimate realization of the art of the sword with the help of the deity of this temple. Nothing happened, and when the last night came, he was desperate. At that point, suddenly he felt in his back an intent to attack and, without thinking, struck horizontally behind him with his sword. He found his enemy dead, sword in hand. He named this technique, which became the highest stage of development within his school, "the sword of emptiness," or nonthought. This story illustrates the importance of emptiness in the art of the sword.

Here is the history of Ito Ittosai's life as it is told in the collection called *Little Anecdotes of the Japanese Martial Arts*, a text from the end of the seventeenth century. In this text we find many facts concerning the great masters:

> Ito Ittosai, a native of the Izu region, studied the spear at the Chu-Jo school with Master Kanemaki Jisai and reached the highest level of accomplishment in this school. He traveled throughout Japan and fought thirty-three times with different swordsmen. His level was like that of a god and impossible to describe. The place of his death is not known. To transmit the secret of the highest technique of his school, he had to choose between his two best disciples, Zenki and Tenzen. He asked them to fight, and Zenki was killed. Then Ittosai transmitted the secret technique (kame wari to) to Tenzen.

After Zenki and Tenzen, Kotoda Toshinao was the disciple of the highest level. His grandson, Kotoda Yahei, drawing on his memories of his grandfather and the teachings his grandfather had received from Ittosai, published *Ittosai Sensei Kempo Sho* (Writings on Sword Master Ito Ittosai,) which is the only document that exists about the teachings of this master. Here are a few passages from this text, which is a particularly difficult one, even in Japanese:

> In our school, technique is fundamental. The techniques are based on reasons. Therefore, it is first necessary to learn the techniques, that is, various actions of the body and mind. Then it is necessary to understand well the reasons that cause

the techniques to vary in accordance with the actions of the adversary. If one trains sufficiently in the techniques without understanding the reasons, victory is never sure. When one understands the reasons well and has trained sufficiently, the reasons that one has understood through the mind will be reflected in the techniques. Then the reasons and the techniques will form a unity, and there will no longer be any difference between the reasons and the techniques. However, in learning the sword, there are people who confine themselves to technical training without learning the reasons; and there are others who seek to understand the reasons without acquiring the techniques. Neither one of these approaches allows one to react appropriately and freely against the adversary.

From the time of Master Ittosai, throughout the history of the development of the art of the sword in our school, disciples have transmitted the secret techniques. These make it possible to execute fully the movements of the sword and of the mind that understands techniques and reasons. I have learned the techniques, but lacking talent, I have not been able to comprehend well the difficult reasons. Nonetheless, because of the ardent requests of my students, I intend to write down what I have learned. This is a little like looking at the vast sky through the opening of a narrow bamboo tube.

In the course of training in the sword, everybody has to understand the causes of his defeat and the reasons for which he was not able to win. The causes of his defeat are the causes of the victory of the adversary; therefore the reasons that prevent him from winning correspond to a very solid defense on the part of the adversary. He who tries only to win [is no other than he who] thus misunderstands the causes of his defeat. One who tries to win while having within himself the causes of his defeat will not be able to discover what constitutes the superiority of his opponent. If one does not try for victory at all costs, there will be no defeat. At the same time, someone who does not know in his mind what defeat is cannot win. In the shadow of absolute victory dwells absolute defeat. And absolute defeat contains absolute victory. A true adept of the sword learns what the defeat in his victory is and what the victory in his defeat is. He develops the techniques and the reasons in himself and reacts in response to the adversary by comprehending the adversary's techniques and reasons.

Chuang Tzu says, "When one knows the adversary and oneself, one can fight a hundred times without danger. When one knows oneself without knowing the adversary, sometimes one wins, sometimes one loses. When one knows neither oneself nor the adversary, one always loses."

Dignity is the state of the man who has prepared himself correctly and who is not troubled by the actions of others. It does not change with the external situation. Dignity overcomes the adversary without action. By contrast, impetuosity overcomes the adversary through action. Dignity is calm, but understands thousands of situations through movement. That is why it is necessary to face the adversary with dignity and go on to victory with impetuosity. Dignity and impetuosity are two different things, but as to the essential, they constitute one single thing. When one reaches the point of not being subject to the influence of the adversary, dignity fills one's body, one is not afraid of him, one does not doubt oneself, and impetuosity is present in the dignity itself. As Lao Tzu says, "Everything is done without doing anything. . . .

There is a sickness in the way of the sword: the reasons precede the techniques, and the postures of the body are determined before the movement of the sword. This sickness comes about when one looks for the techniques and the reasons elsewhere than in one's training. Since the techniques correspond appropriately to the changes in the situation and do not come from reflection, they arise by riding the reasons of nature and they vary and adjust without any reflection. . . .

When one attains the ultimate state, it becomes useless to be attentive to one's mind. The actions of the mind and of the body become one, and there is no difference between good and evil. The actions of the sword, which vary without limit, belong to the mind, and so one can react appropriately to any situation. This is the state that one attains at the end by using one's own mind to go beyond the techniques that have been handed down.

As concerns training, so that tactics don't precede the techniques, it is necessary to keep the mind empty, without letting any irrelevant thoughts arise; then, like the moon reflected in water, one comes to be able to react to any circumstance. Just as water has no rigid form but takes on that of a round or square vessel or any container, training must not be molded into a rigid form, and the movements of the sword must precede the postures of the body. The way of the sword is nothing other than attaining victory with the sword; that is why the art of the sword contains techniques that are based on reasons. The mind is the foundation of the techniques; the postures of the body are the foundations of the movements of the sword.

In general, what is essential is in the background, the details are on the surface, and this is what allows one to win without fail. But when the details are in the background and what is essential is in the foreground, victory can only be won by chance. . . . Thus it is necessary to perfect oneself in the essential and train in the details. . . .

There are two ways to forestall the adversary, by tai and by yu. The first, tai, means to maintain a posture without changing it, then attack. The second, yu, means to change the posture in accordance with the situation and attack by seizing the moment. The master gave the following explanation: When one is forestalling the adversary through tai, one attacks from a constant posture, and for defense, one reacts according to the situation so as to counter the tactics of the adversary. While securely maintaining one's defense, one attacks head-on. In that case, tactics are the essential and techniques are secondary. When one is forestalling the adversary through yu, one attacks with quite varied postures, but one defends oneself with a constant posture; thus one destroys the defense of the adversary and counters his techniques, and then one's attack comes from fairly far away. In this case, technique is essential and tactics become secondary. If, in relation to attack and defense, one does not distinguish between the techniques and reasons of tai and yu and if one pushes oneself to attack in order to gain the victory, it is like holding out one's neck or hand to be cut off. One must train well.

We do not know exactly whether the notions of tai and yu come from Buddhism or from Confucianism, but they played a very important role in the theoretical development of both of them. In brief, we could say that tai is something fundamental and essential, and that ontologically yu comes later. The same relationship exists between tai and yu as between water and waves. In Japan, these notions appear both in the techniques of the martial arts and in the ideology of the warriors. The author we are translating applies these notions to the martial arts in a rather subjective fashion:

There are two ways to defend oneself against the attacks of the adversary, through tai or through yu. When the adversary attacks in tai, one must dismantle his attacks by following his postures. When the adversary does not attack with his full capacity, one reacts against his techniques; and when he attacks with his full capacity, it is necessary to deal with the essential. Against an adversary whose mind is disturbed but appears calm on the surface, one must attack the disturbed point in his mind. Against an adversary whose mind is solid but whose posture is unsettled, one must attack but without putting one's full force into it. Against an adversary whose mind and posture are both disturbed, one must attack taking advantage of the void in him. Against an adversary who is troubled in neither mind nor posture, one must wait until a void comes about in him. But in any case, if one tries to follow the adversary's movements by adapting to his changes in posture, one is in danger of losing one's subjective thread. It is impossible to win by awaiting the adversary's attack if one's technique and one's reasons are disturbed or dominated by the adversary's initiative. The technique in our school for attacking by following the adversary is to nullify his attack by making a counterattack at the moment when his posture changes. To counter the adversary, one reacts with the techniques of tai. To prevent the adversary from making changes, one follows the techniques of yu. One beats the adversary down by countering, and by beating him down, one counters him. In the course of training one learns the movements of the sword and the force of blows, the basic techniques and their application, and the positions of the sword in relation to the body; and when the movements of the sword and those of the mind become unified, one finally reaches the point of being able to use the techniques freely. The reasons are extremely subtle and difficult to communicate. They must be transmitted from mind to mind. One must come to understand these reasons in the same way as one experiences the temperature of water in drinking it.

The most important thing in combat is the ma [distance]. If I have a technique, the adversary has one too; when I attack, he also wants to attack. It is accuracy in gauging distance that determines the outcome of the combat.

In our school, the term *ma* refers to the relationship between the force and the rhythm of combat. One can easily take the initiative in the course of combat if one is capable of penetrating as far as the adversary without allowing any void, be it only a hair's breadth in size. If our mind remains fixed on the ma, we cannot react freely. We must establish our distance appropriately without fixing our mind on it. Thus, without keeping the ma in our mind nor the mind focused on the ma, we must reach the state of the moon on water. The state of the moon on water is the state in which the mind goes beyond the techniques and the reasons. If one makes an attempt to reach this, it will not be the moon on water. When one removes the clouds from the mind, it will become clear, the moon will appear on the water and make us capable of everything. . . . For our school, ma is not only distance; the essence of ma consists in taking the initiative against the adversary without being attached to the distance but rather by grasping the situation of the combat. If as a result of a momentary impulse, one forgets this text, it will amount to the same thing as wounding oneself with one's own sword.

What I call "the parrot technique" is making the techniques the adversary intends to use one's own. When the adversary attacks strongly, one responds strongly; when he attacks mildly, one responds mildly; when he attacks, one parries; when he shows the intention of blocking, one deflects one's own attack. Thus one chooses one's tactic by following that of the adversary. When the adversary attacks in a straightforward spirit, one responds head-on; and when the adversary feigns a void, one reacts with a feint; when the adversary makes a show of weakness when his capacity is great, one does the same thing. Sometimes one feigns a weakness by hiding one's true strength, sometimes one attacks making the adversary believe that the attack is a feint, sometimes one intentionally makes a show of an absurd fault with the aim of doing something else. "Combat is the way of deception," Chuang Tzu writes very accurately. Combat unfolds according to the rule of nature—one must conform to this reason; and the adversary, just like ourselves, reacts according to his abilities. The rule in combat is not that of spontaneity without training. Spontaneity should be heightened by training to such a level that one is spontaneously in conformity with the rule of nature in everyday life.

One of the contemporaries of Katoda Yahei, Harigatani Yuun, sought a result of combat that went completely beyond victory and defeat. For him, the ultimate stage of combat was *ainuke*, a situation in which neither of the two combatants was able to kill the other and in which there was no victory or defeat for either of them. Fundamentally, for him, the ideology of the way of the sword in which the adversary is killed is not separate from an ideology that aims at transcending both victory and defeat in combat.

MIYAMOTO MUSASHI

Miyamoto Musashi (1584–1646) was a legendary master of the sword. At the age of thirteen, he faced Arima Kihei, a seasoned warrior, with a bokken (wooden sword) and killed him. At the age of sixteen he used a sword to kill Akiyama, a warrior known for his strength. During his youth, from ages thirteen to twenty-nine, he fought more than sixty times, on some occasions against several adversaries, and won every time.

He wrote,

At the age of thirty years, I looked at myself critically, and I thought that, though I had achieved victory, it was not because I had reached the ultimate state of the Way, but without doubt because of the fact that my skill was in agreement with universal reason or because of the inadequate level of my adversaries. I trained every day from morning till night, and it was around the age of fifty that I found myself on the way [do] of strategy of the martial art [of the sword]. At this moment I found myself at the very end of this Way. And this permitted me to be a master in all the realms of the arts.

Treading profoundly on the Way
I found myself at the end of the mountains
Near a village.

Musashi founded a school of swordsmanship in which combatants fought with two swords at a time. Normally, samurai carried two swords, a big one and a shorter one, but they used only one sword to fight with. Musashi's combats against the Yoshioka family (illustrious masters of the sword from the Kyoto region), and against Sasaki Kojiro are famous and the story of them has been told more than once in popular literature. Musashi first fought with a wooden sword against the sword master Yoshioka Seijuro. Seijuro lost and had to renounce the sword. His younger brother, Denshichiro, wanted to avenge him. He fought Musashi with a wooden sword more than a meter and a half (more than five feet) in length and was killed. The youngest brother, Matashichiro, had many disciples in his school trained in all the martial arts. He pursued the vendetta against Musashi. Deployed like an army, he and his disciples awaited a confrontation with Musashi. Musashi fought with all his strategic resources. First he killed Matashichiro, then he fled as he fought against Matashichiro's men, taking advantage of the least details of the terrain. I will not repeat here the minute description of the fight as given in various novels, but even if it is quite exaggerated, this anecdote conveys Musashi's skill in defending himself against multiple adversaries.

Sasaki Kojiro was a sword master whose skill stood in the highest repute. The duel between Musashi and Kojiro took place on a tiny deserted island south of Japan. Musashi arrived later than the appointed hour in a small fishing boat. As the boat was crossing to the site of the duel, Musashi made a long wooden sword out of an oar. He approached the place of combat with the sun at his back. Kojiro was waiting for him, irritated by his lateness. Upon Musashi's arrival, Kojiro drew a very long sword from its sheath. Musashi leaped from the boat into knee-deep water, plunging the end of his sword into the water in order to hide its length. He advanced, back to the sun. The combat was short. Koshiro had no way of gauging the length of Musashi's sword, which, cut from an oar, was well longer than usual. Koshiro was killed on his first assault by a blow struck to the middle of his forehead. Some people have taken a critical view of Musashi's tactic, saying that because of Kojiro's extreme skill with the sword, Musashi had been uncertain he could using genuine sword techniques and so had resorted to a trick.

Musashi spent a great part of his life traveling in order to perfect his art. He fought many swordsmen. He only taught for a few years, broken into two periods—when he was around forty and then again at the end of his life, when he was welcomed at the courts of the great feudal lords.

He also practiced other arts besides the sword and attained a very high level in calligraphy, painting, poetry, sculpture, and tea ceremony. Despite his renown, his teaching remained strongly associated with him personally and did not outlast his death. Musashi felt that his art was applicable to combat in large numbers and would have liked to apply his theory and abilities as a leader of armies. But the time he lived in was the one in which the wars came to an end, when peace was established and bureaucracy came to rule the day. Thus he never had the opportunity to develop his abilities as a general or to attain the corresponding social rank. This is why, in spite of the improvements he had brought to the art of the sword, his teaching did not produce a lasting school, as had, for example, the Yagyu school. Nonetheless, following his death, his written works were read by many swordsmen.

Musashi died at the age of sixty-two. He wrote several works, of which the last, written when he was sixty years old, is considered the most pithy formulation of his thought. This work, the *Go Rin No Sho* (literally, "Writings of the Five Wheels") is composed of five scrolls. The first, the Scroll of Earth, presents the general system of his school. The Scroll of Water primarily describes its techniques. The Scroll of Fire applies Musashi's principles to military strategy. The Scroll of Wind critiques the other schools. And the Scroll of Sky (or Scroll of Space), which is very short, presents his conclusions. The organization of the work is not as rigorous as this systematic presentation might lead one to think.

I will begin by presenting excerpts from the Scroll of Earth, the Scroll of Water, and the Scroll of Fire, following the general order used by Musashi but bringing together texts relative to the same themes (certain themes are repeated often in these three scrolls).

The Scroll of Earth

In my school, from the beginning, we train with two swords in our hands. When one is fighting for one's life, one must make use of everything one has. It would be regrettable to die with a sword in one's belt without ever using it; but it is very difficult to smoothly employ a sword in each hand. That is why we train from the beginning to use the large sword with just one hand. One needs two hands to hold a spear or a *naginata*,[5] but one can hold either the large or the small sword in one hand. It is very awkward to hold the long sword with two hands while on horseback or when running over terrain that is marshy, stony, or very steep, or again in a place where there are many people. Also one is forced to hold the sword in just one hand when one is carrying a bow or a spear in the left hand. Thus holding the sword in two hands is not a fundamental element of the art of the sword. When one cannot kill the adversary with one hand, one must use two hands. These are simple things. Two swords should be carried with the goal of learning to use one sword with each hand. In the beginning, everyone experiences difficulty using the sword with one hand, because it is very heavy; but as a result of training fortified by the Way, it becomes easier. It is the same with archery, the naginata, and so on.

CONCERNING HYOSHI IN
THE ART OF THE SWORD

Hyoshi is found in all things, but in the art of the sword, it is impossible to acquire without training. Hyoshis exist also in the ways of dance and music, but they are concordant hyoshis. In the way of the martial arts, there are particular hyoshis for archery, rifle shooting, and equitation. Hyoshi is important in the various crafts. In the art of the sword, hyoshi exists in several forms. It is very important to learn about concordant hyoshi and then about discordant hyoshi. And it is important among the great and small, and slow and fast hyoshis, to distinguish concordant hyoshi, the hyoshi of ma [interval of distance], and discordant hyoshi. This last is essential; if it is missing, your sword will not be sure. In combat, knowing the hyoshi of the adversary, I must utilize a hyoshi that does not even occur to him, and I will be victorious by bringing forth the hyoshi of emptiness from the hyoshi of wisdom.

The Scroll of Water

CONCERNING STATE OF MIND
IN THE ART OF THE SWORD

One's state of mind during combat need not be different from one's ordinary state of mind. In daily life as well as in combat, one must keep one's mind open and straight, neither too tight nor too loose, nor off center. One must place one's mind in the center and move it gently, even at moments when one is off balance. One must train well in all that. When the body is calm, the mind does not stop, and when the body is moving quite violently, the mind remains calm. The mind must not be carried away by the body nor the body by the mind. . . . The mind must be cautious when the body is bold. The mind must be full, but not at all spill over. When the surface of the mind appears weak, the depths of the mind must be solid so that the adversary does not perceive its true state. Those who are small (either in size or in number) must know well those who are big (either in size or in number), and the big and the small alike must keep their minds straight without either overestimating or underestimating.

In the art of the sword, one's way of looking must be big and broad. One must be able to distinguish between looking (one's glance goes deep, to the essence of things) and seeing (one's glance apprehends the surface of things). Looking is essential, seeing is insufficient. One must look at what is distant as though it were close and at what is close as though it were distant. I want to stress this point. It is important to perceive the adversary's sword without looking at it, whether during a duel or in a combat involving numerous adversaries. It is necessary to look at both sides without moving one's eyes, but it is not possible to acquire this ability right away. Having understood what I have just written, one must accustom oneself to look all the time in this manner so as to become capable of maintaining this way of looking in any situation.

CONCERNING THE MANNER OF HOLDING THE SWORD

One grasps the sword, keeping a certain flexibility in the thumb and index finger, with the middle finger neither too tight nor too loose, and with the fourth finger and the little finger quite tight. It is very harmful to have a void in the middle of the hand. One must grasp the sword with the spirit of cutting the adversary in two. When one cuts the adversary down, the form of the hand does not change. When one parries, whether one is pressing against the adversary's sword or blocking, only the index finger and the thumb move slightly. In any case, when one grasps the sword, it is with the spirit of cutting the adversary through.

CONCERNING THE MANNER
OF MOVING THE FEET

One must place one's foot by at first putting down the heel with force and keeping the toes slightly raised. According to the situation, one moves the feet a lot or a little, slowly or fast, but always with a walking rhythm. Three ways of moving the feet are distinguished: leaping, sliding (with the foot slightly lifted), and pressing down hard; but it is important not to move only one foot. When one cuts, when one backs up, and when one parries, one must always move the right foot and the left. One must train well.

CONCERNING THE PRINCIPLE
OF SWORD MOVEMENT

If one has properly acquired the principle of sword movement, then one reaches the point of using the sword with only two fingers. If one tries to move one's sword very fast, one violates the principle and one encounters difficulties. The sword must be moved calmly and correctly. When one uses the sword as quickly as a fan or a small knife, one cannot cut a man down. When one strikes from above down or horizontally, one brings back the sword in accordance with the discipline, with the arms properly deployed and with an ample movement.

Musashi goes on to give a detailed exposition of five techniques of combat. These principles are of major significance for karate. Once one has acquired the techniques of defense and attack, of punches and kicks, the problem becomes knowing how to use these techniques. At the present time in karate circles, there is a tendency to prioritize speed and superficial dynamics. The foregoing description by Musashi is very loaded with meaning in this respect, but for people who have not really acquired the techniques, there is no question yet of applying them. They do not yet possess a sufficiently effective "sword."

CONCERNING THE GUARD
WITHOUT A GUARD

In swordsmanship, fundamentally, there is no guard position but rather five main ways of holding the sword. Thus it could be said that there are five guards. The manner in which one holds the sword is a function of the situation in which one enters the relationship with one's adversary, the goal being to cut him down. When one takes the high guard (jodan), if one then lowers one's sword a little, that becomes the middle-level guard (chudan); and if one raises the sword again from this position, that again becomes the high guard. The same goes for [raising the sword from] the low guard (gedan); and when one holds the sword to the right or to the left: by changing levels one moves to the high, middle, or low guard. That is why I speak of a guard without a guard.

Musashi writes elsewhere,

In any case, the fundamental guard is that of the middle level (chudan), and the other four are nothing but variants. Once one takes up the sword, the goal is to cut the adversary in two. If one parries, strikes, touches, clings to, rubs on, or grazes the sword of the adversary, it is to create an opportunity to cut him down. If one makes these movements for their own sake, it will be very difficult to cut the adversary down. All these movements serve to create an opportunity. One must train in this well.

In karate also, dodges and various blocks exist, but from the point of view of tactics, you should not use these movements for their own sake. These movements create the opportunity for counterattacks, and at the ultimate level, the dodges and the blocks themselves contain the means of dominating your opponent.

CONCERNING A HYOSHI
FOR STRIKING THE ADVERSARY

This is a hyoshi that is utilized when one is at a distance from the adversary at which he can be attacked. It is a hyoshi with which one strikes the adversary without moving one's body and with the mind immobile. One strikes with a single blow quickly at the instant in which the adversary is undecided whether to draw back his sword, to move it sideways, or to attack. One must learn this ma hyoshi well and train well at executing it quickly.

CONCERNING THE NI NO KOCHI NO HYOSHI[6]

When one is just about to launch an attack, if the adversary already telegraphs a movement of backing up or parrying, one pretends to strike, and if the adversary reacts by tensing up, one strikes a little bit later, seizing the moment at which he relaxes. It is very difficult to communicate this technique in writing, but it is easy when shown directly.

CONCERNING THE SEKKA STRIKE
(STONE AND SPARK)

At a distance at which the adversary's sword and my own barely touch, I strike extremely hard without at all raising my sword. . . . To execute this technique, one must have strength in the legs, the body, and the hands. With these three strengths, one strikes. This strike is difficult to execute if one is not sufficiently trained.

Musashi here gives a simple description of a technique that is extremely difficult. Anyone who has practiced the sword, even a little, will understand that this simplicity shows to what extent Musashi has mastered the physical techniques as well as the more profound aspects of his art.

CONCERNING DEFLECTED BLOWS AND CHANCE BLOWS

When you strike, it is necessary to distinguish clearly whether you are doing so intentionally or by chance. When you strike intentionally, no matter what kind of a blow it is, it is delivered with a confident mind; but a chance blow is delivered accidentally, and even if you strike very hard and the adversary dies from the blow, it is by chance. You should think this over well.

CONCERNING THE TECHNIQUE "WITH THE BODY OF SUKHO"[7]

Before striking the adversary, you move your entire body forward, as though you were not using your arms. When one intends to extend one's arms in the direction of the adversary, the body recoils backward instinctively. That is why it is necessary to move the body forward first.

THE BODY LIKE LACQUER

Having approached very close to the adversary, it occurs to you not to pull away from him, but stay glued to him like a coat of lacquer. You stay close to him with the head, the body, the feet, everything. Usually in combat, there is a tendency to put the head and feet forward, while the hips move farther away. Therefore it is necessary to glue the whole body to him like lacquer, without any gap. You must reflect on this.

CONCERNING MOVING THE WHOLE BODY FORWARD

This is a technique in which you give the adversary's body a violent shock. You put your left shoulder forward and strike the adversary violently in the chest with it, slightly turning your head aside. You deliver this blow gathering together your whole force, using the hyoshi of the breath. If this technique has been well learned, the adversary will be thrown back four to six meters [yards], or maybe he will die instantly. You must train well.

CONCERNING THE THREE PARRIES

The first makes it possible to parry if the adversary attacks when I am advancing toward him. I block the sword of the adversary by deflecting it over my right shoulder with my sword, which I direct toward his eye. The second is a block using the point. I block the adversary's sword by stabbing mine in the direction of his right eye, with the blade of my sword positioned as though I were going to slash his neck. The third takes place when the adversary attacks. I block with the small sword held in my left hand, moving forward without paying heed to the length of the blade—as though I were going to strike the adversary's face with my left fist.

Often writings on the art of the sword from this period suggest that in order to deliver the right blow in combat, you must direct your attack as though you were aiming to strike with the wrist or the hilt of the sword. Musashi's third parry fits this approach. In traditional karate training, you control blows to the vital points by halting them at a distance of one to three centimeters [.39 to 1.1

inches]. One superficial criticism concludes from this that karate is not effective, because with this method you would not be capable of landing a blow in a case of necessity, since you do not practice doing so in training. Based on this criticism, a tendency has developed in sports karate to train without control. But this criticism is false, because the controlled movement is not a movement that ends naturally at its stopping point. If you are aiming to strike a vital point in the belly, for example, the move is launched as though to hit a point beyond that, somewhere in the back, and the action of control consists in blocking this move in the middle of its trajectory. This makes objective evaluation of the quality of the blows extremely difficult. For those training in combat, the mind-set that one is delivering blows that go as far as to be life-threatening but are controlled is exactly what constitutes the quality of one's work. Karate in the West has fallen under the influence of sports to the extent that only the objective aspect is taken into account. This corresponds to criteria related to visible form, dynamism, and so on. But the subjective aspect that constitutes the real effectiveness of budo has not been adequately developed.

It should be well understood that just the fact that this aspect is subjective does not make it entirely individual. That is what makes it possible to judge a match in which there is no contact. The referee understands that the quality of the controlled blow can only be based on a certain level of intersubjective communication that in turn must be based on the referee's personal practice of this type of control. Moreover, if the level of quality is sufficient, the combatant knows that he has lost without having been struck by the blow, or he knows that he has won without his blow having landed; and it is solely on the basis of his own practice that the referee can enter into this relationship and make a judgment. This condition is very difficult to fulfill. This is the reason that combat on a high level is not always spectacular and is difficult for people without sufficient practice to evaluate. It's not like at the movies.

Musashi goes on to describe various blocking techniques:

CONCERNING COMBAT AGAINST
SEVERAL ADVERSARIES

When you fight against several persons, you draw the big and the small swords, with the arms broadly deployed to the right and the left. When your adversaries attack from four sides, you have to fight by drawing them into a single direction; so, distinguishing well which of them is closest and which farther back, you fight first with the one who is closest. You must keep your field of vision very broad, perceive precisely the moment to attack, and strike in two different directions, using both swords at the same time. You must not stop after having struck, but return immediately to your starting position. When your adversaries approach, cut with force the one who is closest. At all costs, you must keep your adversaries one behind the other like dried fish on a string. As soon as your adversaries make a frontal attack, destroy their order with force. It is not good to attack adversaries in a compact group nor to wait to react until your adversaries advance.

You must gain victory by apprehending the hyoshi of the adversaries and by finding moments of instability in them. From time to time, it is necessary to train against numerous adversaries, directing their actions. This way you know what fighting against several persons is, and combat against ten or twenty persons becomes as certain as combat against just one. You must train and reflect well.

The Scroll of Fire

CONCERNING THE TERRAIN OF COMBAT

In combat, you must place yourself with your back to the sun; and if you can't do that, place yourself with the sun on your right. If you are fighting indoors, place yourself with your back to the light or with the light on your right.

You must have a big enough space behind you so that you can move around without obstacle. It is desirable to have room on your left, even if it means being more squeezed on the right.

At night, if you can see your adversary, you should place yourself with the lantern behind you or to your right. It is also very important to occupy the higher ground.

Musashi next describes several techniques that make it possible to regain the initiative of attack at a moment when the adversary has begun to attack; at the same time he indicates that it is very difficult to convey these techniques by written means:

CONCERNING TRAMPLING ON THE ADVERSARY'S SWORD

Also when fighting a single adversary [Musashi has first explained how to use this technique against several adversaries], if one replies in turn to each of his strokes, the result of the combat will be dubious, because the rhythm will become repetitive. Thus, with the spirit of trampling on the sword the adversary is deploying, I prevent it from striking another blow against me. I trample on it not only with my feet but with my body, my mind, and of course with my sword. This is not crashing into the adversary from the front, but following his movement in order to prevent it. You must reflect well on this.

For me "following the movement" of the adversary "in order to prevent it" means taking the initiative by changing the cadence.

CONCERNING MAKING THE SHADOW MOVE

When I do not see the mind of the adversary, I make his shadow move. In combat against several persons or in war, if I cannot make out what the adversary is going to do, I make a show of attacking very hard and I observe his tactic. His tactic being unveiled, the combat becomes easier. In a combat of two, if I cannot make out the tactic of the adversary, whether he is holding his sword to the rear or to the side, I suddenly pretend to attack, and then his mind is reflected by his sword. I reply in accordance with his tactic, and I defeat him with certainty. But the least lapse will make me miss the decisive hyoshi. You must reflect on this well.

CONCERNING CONTAGION

Many things are contagious—sleep, yawning, and also mood.

In war, when the enemy is excited or in a hurry, make a show of acting gently, calmly, and slowly. The enemy will be influenced and his mind will relax. At the moment when we judge his mind to be relaxed, we should attack with force and speed, anticipating his counterattacks and having the mind of emptiness.

The same goes for a combat between two persons. I make myself slow and gentle, in body as well as mind; I induce the adversary to relax, and at the moment when he relaxes, I attack with force and speed, anticipating him, and I defeat him.

There is another technique that is rather similar, called "intoxicating." You cause the adversary to get irritated or to have a mind that is drifting or weak. You should reflect on this well.

CONCERNING THE THREE VOICES (KIAI)

In war, three voice registers are used, one for the beginning, another for the middle, and another for the end. . . .

At the beginning of the combat, the voice is exaggerated, during the battle it is low and should seem deep, and finally, after the victory, the voice is strong and raised. In a fight be-

tween two combatants, in order to make the adversary move,
I make a show of attacking while letting out a *kiai-ei*; then I
strike. After having struck the adversary, I let out a kiai in
order to announce my victory. I do not let out the cry with
force at the same time as I am moving my sword; during the
combat, cry out low and lightly in order to lean into the hyoshis. You must reflect on this well.

CONCERNING "RAISING THE BOTTOM"

During the combat, it can happen that you are winning from
a technical point of view, but at bottom, the adversary is not
completely defeated.

At this point, you must renew your will and annihilate the
adversary's mind in order to convince him that he is completely defeated. I explode his bottom with my sword as well
as with my body and my mind. It is only when the adversary
is defeated from the bottom up that I can cease keeping my
mind alert. . . .

You must train well for fighting against one adversary and
against several.

The Scroll of Wind

I will cite here several important passages of Musashi's critique of
concepts of the art that differ from his.

His first criticism is of those who emphasize choosing the
longest sword, because that tends to mask a weakness in their level
of accomplishment, and because in actual combat, circumstances
vary: in a narrow space or when very close, you cannot use a long
sword. What is important is to know in what circumstances to
use a long or short sword. You should be able to use a very long
sword, but you must avoid limiting your thinking to the length of
your sword.

He criticizes the emphasis that some put on the strength of the blow:

A strong or weak stroke should not exist in swordsmanship. The blow that is struck with the intention of landing the strongest blow quite possibly becomes crude, and when your sword becomes crude, it is difficult to win.

What cuts well is not force. Musashi writes, "When you are fighting for your life, you do not cut with the intention of striking with more or less force, you strike to kill your adversary."
He criticizes the tendency to proliferate techniques:

Teaching a multitude of techniques tends toward commercialization of the art of the sword. It serves to convince beginners that you know a lot of techniques. This is wrong, because it false to think that there are a lot of techniques for cutting a man in two.

Then he writes that the fundamental function of the sword does not change:

Whether it is held by an adept, a woman, or a child, its use is to cut—by bearing down, pulling, or pushing—or to penetrate. But in accordance with the place or the circumstances of combat, so that the sword does not encounter any obstacles, we make use of five guard positions. Apart from that, cutting a man by twisting the wrist or the body or by jumping are not what we should try for. . . . According to my teaching, you should induce the adversary to twist himself into an awkward position, and then when his mind is twisted, you defeat him by keeping your body and mind straight.

He criticizes the way various schools recommend directing the eyes:

Depending on the school, some keep their eyes on the sword, others on the hand, the face, or the feet. But fixing the gaze on one spot, whatever it is, tends to be disconcerting. . . . When one achieves the way of the sword, one reaches the point of seeing everything: position, distance, and speed. What you must look at is the mind of the adversary.

He criticizes those who mainly seek speed:

That is not a certain path. What people call speed is in reality not being in tune with the hyoshi of all things. The movements of true experts do not appear rapid. In dance or in singing, when an expert and beginner dance or sing together, the beginner always has the feeling of coming in late, and his mind becomes hasty. The expert who taps in rhythm on the drum does it calmly, whereas the beginner always thinks he is lagging behind. . . . Rapidity is in fact discord with regard to the ma [understood here in the sense of a temporal interval in a cadence]. The movement of a true expert looks rather slow, but the ma is satisfied, and he never looks rushed. This phenomenon should be understood well from this example. When you try to cut fast, the sword does not cut very well— it is neither a fan nor a small knife.

He criticizes differentiating between technique of beginners and technique for more advanced swordsmen:

Certain schools distinguish between technique for beginners and secret or ultimate techniques. But when talking about real combat, it makes no sense to say, "I fought with a beginner's technique or with a secret technique." In the teaching of my school, I have a beginner work on techniques and ideas that are easy to learn, and as his mind broadens, I teach him corresponding techniques and reasons. One learns what is necessary according to one's level of progress, and I do not distinguish between techniques for beginners and techniques for more advanced swordsmen. . . . He who has entered the deepest part of the dense forest [an image for seeking accomplishment in budo] will reach the end of the forest and come out on the other side. It is not necessary in the way of the martial arts to keep a technique secret.

What Musashi says is true for all the martial arts, including karate. There is no secret to be kept. A practitioner who has confidence in his level of accomplishment can show everything he knows. His force resides in being able to make the skill he has acquired function in accordance with circumstances. That which constitutes quality is not something that can be learned at a glance.

The Scroll of Sky (or Emptiness)

What I write here is the essence of my teaching on swordsmanship. Emptiness means that nothing exists, and that "nothing" cannot be the object of knowledge. Emptiness is not equal to anything existing. True emptiness is not merely knowing something that does not exist—that is just errant mind. Some who practice swordsmanship without knowing what the Way is speak of emptiness when they arrive at an impasse. This is not true emptiness. The bushi [samurai] must learn the way of the sword with certainty and also train in the other martial arts to perfect his actions and eliminate trouble from his mind; he should not stop his training after a day or an hour. He must polish his mind, his will, his insight, and his ability to observe. Thus, with every cloud of trouble gone, the sky is clear, and that is true emptiness.

Musashi next explains that often one thinks one is on the right path, but that this is not true if one has not reached this stage—the ultimate goal of swordsmanship is to attain true emptiness. The end of development in the art of the sword is emptiness.

> In the state of emptiness, there is no good and there is no evil. When one has attained the wisdom, the reason, and the mind of swordsmanship, one can arrive at the mind of emptiness.

ISSAI CHOZANSHI

Niwa Jurozaemon was a sword master also known under the pseudonym Issai Chozanshi. He studied Zen and Confucianism and was the author of several written works. He followed the way of the sword throughout his life.

Here I will present excerpts from his book *Tengu Gei Jutsu Ron*, written in 1729.

It will help the reader understand the context of this book to summarize an ancient Japanese legend. There was a young man who had been training for a very long time in the art of swordsmanship but had not yet attained the ultimate state. He heard the following story. One day an ancient master of the sword went deep into the mountain wilds and met there the god Tengu, who was well versed in the martial arts.[8] Hearing this, the young man also wanted to be instructed by this god. So he too went deep into the mountains and each night he seated himself on a rock and invoked Tengu. One night, along with appalling noise and violent wind, the god arrived from the sky and landed in a very tall cedar. He replied to the young man's questions. The book relates the conversation between the god and the young swordsman. The god first expounds the basics of the martial arts and then replies to the young man's questions.

> As you make progress in the techniques, the body and the mind merge into a unity. Then the reasons contained in the

techniques occur to you. When a technique is perfectly as-similated, the technique and the reason form a unity, the mind becomes absolutely stable and moves freely. This is the traditional way of learning the martial arts. That is why, for making progress in budo, training is the most important thing. Without ripening the techniques, there is no unifica-tion of mind and body. And if body and mind do not become unified, one's movements lag and one cannot react smoothly.

IT IS SAID THAT GREAT MASTERS OF THE SWORD HAVE REACHED THE ULTIMATE STATE BY MEETING A ZEN MONK. WHY?

The Zen monk did not show them the ultimate state of swordsmanship. When the mind is fulfilled, one can react cor-rectly to whatever comes along; by contrast, if one attacks life too much, one torments oneself, one is filled with anxiety and unrest, which puts one's life in danger. These masters trained continuously in the sword for many years; even using their sleep time for practice, they forged their spirit, polished their technique, and engaged in many combats. They spent many years in their efforts, but without attaining the state of satori. So when they met the Zen monk, the reasons of life and death were illuminated and they understood that all phenomena are only the reflection of the movement of minds. Following that, their problems dissipated. They attained stability of mind by becoming detached from all things, and they reached the point where they could employ the techniques with great ease since, over the years, they had acquired the necessary results of train-ing. They did not reach this state all of a sudden. The same is true when people say they attained satori by being struck by a Zen monk's stick. Those who lack the foundation of the mar-tial arts will not attain the state of satori, even if they meet a very great Zen monk.

I HAVE SEVERAL YOUNG CHILDREN.
HOW SHOULD I TEACH THEM THE SWORD?

Young people, who do not yet have the ability to understand the reasons, should first be taught the physical techniques necessary at their age without too many explanations. First solidity of limb must be developed; then you should accustom them to spiritual training so as to orient them toward learning the ultimate state. This is the process of training. If you teach them at the beginning that the mind of emptiness causes the techniques to arise naturally or that flexibility is more effective than rigidity and force, or that learning the techniques is not fundamental, they will lose the foundation of life and will learn neither physical techniques nor mental techniques.

WHAT ABOUT "MOTIONLESSNESS IN MOTION,
CALM WITHOUT CALM"?

Humans are fundamentally active and cannot remain motionless. In social life, various movements occur, but those who have followed the Way, having become detached, can keep a calm mind without being disturbed by their surroundings. With regard to the sword, for example, if you are surrounded by many enemies fighting you on your right and left and you detach your mind from maintaining your safety, it will be stable and will not fall under the influence of the enemies. This state is called "motionlessness in movement". . . .

What does "calm without calm" mean? When the mind of a man is not influenced by feelings of pleasure, anger, sadness, or joy, his mind is emptied and detached from all things. In this state he can react quite freely to all external changes. Then the essence of the mind does not move and is calm while the actions of the mind carry on freely in accordance with the surroundings. The essence of the mind that remains

motionless understands all the principles and attains uncanny ability; the actions of the mind then follow the principles of the universe and respond correctly to all situations.
Thus "calm without calm" relates at the same time to the essence and to actions. I will now speak of this state of mind in
swordsmanship. Face-to-face with an adversary, the mind is
calm like a deep abyss, without hate, without fear, and without tactics; but when the adversary attacks, it is able to react
very freely. Then the body moves, but the mind does not lose
its essential calm, like a calm and clear mirror in which everything is reflected but which is without a trace when things
disappear. Such is the uncanny force of the essence of the
mind. By contrast, a mediocre man loses his true spirit when
he moves, because he has trained in terms of movements; and
when he becomes calm, he loses his vitality and is not able to
respond to the changes in his surroundings.

WHAT DOES "THE MOON ON WATER" MEAN?

Interpretations vary from one school to another, but basically it symbolizes the empty mind that moves freely.

The Water of Hirosawa Pond
Does not think about reflecting the moon,
Nor does the moon try to be reflected on its water.

You can try to understand the state of emptiness through this
poem. There is only one moon in the sky, but the surface of every
river reflects a moon. If there were no water, the moon would not
be reflected, but it is not the water that creates the moonlight.
The light of the moon does not change if it is reflected by several
rivers, and the size of the moon also does not change. You must
understand the mind through examples. The important thing is
the relationship between the moon and the water and not the
transparency of the water. In any case, the moon has a form and

the mind does not have a form. That is why the example of the moon is given as an aid to understanding.

I DO NOT UNDERSTAND THE INTERPRETATION OF ZANSHIN GIVEN BY SEVERAL SCHOOLS.[9]

This means that you do not move the essence of the mind through the techniques that you practice. If the essence of your mind is solid and stable, you will react faultlessly to whatever arises. The same is true of life. If you deliver a sword blow with the intention of going as deep as the depths of hell with it, your "I" still does not change. Then you are able to move forward and back, to the right or to the left, with all freedom; the mind is not carried away by the will. But this does not mean that you leave a part of your mind alone while you devote the rest to the techniques. If you do that, the mind will divide in two. And if you move without thinking but without having the depths of the mind solid, it is no more than the strike of a blind man. The right decision comes from the mind; it is enough to react by following it. This is difficult to describe in words, and it is dangerous to misunderstand it.

IF I UNDERSTAND CORRECTLY, THE TECHNIQUES OF SWORDSMANSHIP ARISE FROM THE ESSENCE OF THE MIND; BUT THEN WHY DO SECRET TECHNIQUES EXIST?

The principle of swordsmanship is the universal principle. If I can understand it, why couldn't everybody understand it? You keep it secret for the sake of beginners. Beginners would not keep up their motivation if there was no secret. The secret is a means of conveying better understanding. Thus a secret technique is only a partial detail of the technique and is not the essence of it. Unfortunately, since beginners do not have the ability to appreciate certain techniques properly, they understand them badly and transmit them that way.

For this reason it comes about that we only teach techniques to those who can understand them. But as to the essence, we speak openly to everyone, without hiding anything.

MATSUURA SEIZAN

Matsuura Seizan, born in 1760, was the thirty-fourth lord of the Matsuura family. He took over his title at the age of nineteen, and at twenty-seven, he handed over control of his domain to his successor. Thereafter he devoted himself to the martial arts and to literature. He was the author of many essays, and was known for his writing. When he was twenty-six, his school of swordsmanship accepted him into the highest grade. This school, which continued until 1908, was called Shin Kei To Ryu (*shin* meaning "mind"; *kei*, "form" or "technique"; *to*, "sword"; *ryu*, "school"). Seizan interpreted this name by saying that the mind is very important for progress in swordsmanship, but that one begins to shape the mind on the basis of acquiring the techniques. Since Musashi's era, times had changed and sword combats to the death had become much less frequent. This was the middle of the period of peace among the feudal lords. The practice of swordsmanship had become institutionalized and was a mandatory part of the life of warriors. Combat practice in the dojo had taken on major importance. It was done mostly with wooden swords, to which swords of bamboo (*shinai*) were eventually added, as well as special weapons which made it possible to strike blows more freely and develop one's technique.

Here are a few extracts from Seizan's best-known book, *Joseishi Kendan* (Words on Swordsmanship):

Concerning the exercise called *sekkoto* (sword that cuts the steel helmet), one of the techniques of his school, he writes,

In this exercise, you strike downward from above. It is preferable to have the mind empty, not to look at your adversary's sword. You rid yourself of all perceptions as though you are relying on the power of a god; you should not even feel that it is your own movement that strikes. Someone who does not believe in the words of the master never reaches the ultimate state. But someone who believes his master when he says that the sword can defeat artillery will never get there either.

In the art of the sword, there are techniques that make it possible to win by surprise. But this is simply because your adversary does not know swordsmanship sufficiently well. The reason is that the movements of the limbs of the human body are more or less the same for everybody, and there are no unforeseeable movements. The techniques of swordsmanship are the actions of the limbs of the body prolonged by the sword. The sword does not move by itself, it follows the movements of the limbs. That is why, knowing this rule well, if you study those movements minutely, you will come to know both the ordinary techniques and the secret techniques. Even a beginner should reflect well and train as much as possible in combat—that is the way to discover the rules. Here combat does not refer to actual combat to the death; we are talking about combat in the dojo for training purposes. If one who follows the way of the sword is attacked from behind, whether he is drinking sake, talking to a woman, or listening to music, his state of mind will enable him to cut the adversary down. To arrive at this state, it is necessary to spend every day seeking after it.

It is generally thought that one enters upon what is most important in the art of the sword at the moment one begins to exchange blows. But this is only a detail. The most important thing happens before one unsheathes one's sword, before the exchange of blows. You must understand well what that means: for example, a rifle bullet can pass through a hard obstacle with great force, but it is at the end of its trajectory that it passes through the obstacle. True, if the bullet reaches the target, it will pierce anything hard, but if it does not hit the target, that amounts to zero. So it is before firing that the most important moment occurs.

I said, "When you win, there are surprising victories, but when you lose, there are no surprising defeats." My host asked, "Why do you say 'surprising victories'?" I replied, "When you fight following the rule and employing the techniques, you can get the win, even if it is not entirely satisfying. When you think about it afterward, you can say to yourself that it was a surprising victory." My host asked me, "So then why do you say that there is no such thing as a surprising defeat?" I replied, "When you fight neglecting the rules and you make technical errors, you are certain of defeat; that's why I say that."

In general, the secret of sword technique is not meant to be kept for oneself, because if you do not try to apply this technique to training, you cannot use it in real combat.

Therefore when you have had a secret technique communicated to you, you should try to apply it either with your master or with someone who already knows it. After that, you should keep it secret. But a technique that has never been practiced has no value as a secret technique.

Making a comparison between everyday life and theatrical representations, he explains that, on the stage, what is done cannot be redone:

It is the same with the art of the sword. The dojo [preparation] is the background, and everyday life is the foreground. Therefore it is stupid to think that it is enough to do well at the dojo. The dojo is like backstage at the theater, and everyday life is like the stage. On the stage, you cannot redo things, but beforehand you can rehearse as much as you want. People often think the opposite. One often hears talk about

matches between schools and hears the praises of the win-
ners sung. Someone who has received such praise might
think that his technique is superior and that he has really
defeated his adversary. For my part, I do not see it that way.
According to the outlook of our school, a transitory victory is
not a victory in life. Even if you defeat an adversary, that does
not mean that you have beaten him once and for all. . . . Making a judgment about victory on the basis of a transitory result does not make any sense. Victory that lasts throughout
your whole life, the victory that you have won in relation to
your usual mind, is the true victory. Such is the technique of
the art of the sword. A person who follows the way of the
sword and can understand this is worthy of receiving the ultimate technique of our school.

The characteristic traits of the sword technique of each of these
authors reflect the historical period in which they lived. Each one
of them has brought out several important points of the theory—
or rather, the logic—of the art of the sword, but these points are
relatively difficult to bring out clearly because they are permeated
by morality and ideology. Indeed, for these authors, the art of the
sword is intimately linked to religious, ethical, and social values.

However, one point of convergence exists among them all: the
notion of detachment of mind, or "emptiness." But it must be
stressed that, for them, detachment of mind is not a goal in itself.
It lies at the root of their mastery of swordsmanship; it is a state of
mind that they have experienced, a state on the basis of which they
became capable of reacting appropriately in all circumstances.
They have expressed this state and its enabling quality by means of
images in an attempt to transmit the resultant ability in a concrete
way. The way of thinking of this era was not compatible with analytic logic, and this is the source of our own difficulty in penetrating what these authors experienced. I think this is also because
their thinking unfolded in a different way from ours, and that they
consequently developed certain abilities in the direction of which

contemporary thought, pervaded as it is by analytic logic, does not lead. But we should not conclude that this cultural achievement is an archaism. The way of thinking of this period resulted in a development of human abilities that we can seek to achieve today by different paths. Scientific thought should make it possible for us to go beyond the limits the early swordsmen encountered.

In an effort to provide an analysis of the state of detachment in budo, I have interpreted it as a moment in which consciousness moves in "expanded time." This orientation of consciousness can lead to a better level of mastery of the body. The main fruit it bore for these early authors was to make it possible for them to win with certainty in combat. I have tried in this book to analyze what combat in the sense of budo is, and to show where effectiveness in this kind of combat comes from. Concretely speaking, in combat our body moves in a continuous relationship of relative distance and cadence (maai and hyoshi) with regard to an adversary whom we must anticipate (yomi) with certainty. Integrating technical accomplishment with these dimensions is what assures effectiveness in combat.

CONCLUSION

THE IDEA OF KARATE-DO is not to repress oneself by means of a violent physical practice, but rather to balance one's conscious and unconscious mind. One does this by entering into "expanded time" through a practice that is both physical and mental at the same time. Such an activity renews balance on the personal level, but it is evident that in these modern times such a practice can have only a limited effect.

I have therefore proposed karate goshin-do as a development of karate in our contemporary social context that can provide us with a practice that remains both complex and profound. For it is not a question here of maintaining the discipline of budo as an antique relic. Rather, our aim is to achieve a genuine practice of budo by integrating it into a way of life that is fundamentally different from that in which it originated.

A strong tendency exists to view karate as a discipline that leads to a mystical state; but I believe this is a partial vision, indeed a false one.

In this book I have provided a structural analysis of karate-do, not as a sport but as a martial art that had its origin in the culture of the Japanese warriors. I have distinguished three dimensions within it: the dimension of physical technique, the dimension of maai and hyoshi, and the dimension of yomi. These three dimensions form the foundation of most of the Japanese martial arts. If we want to make effective progress on the Way and attain the elevated summit of the martial arts (sought by Japanese adepts of the preindustrial period) by means of intense, experiential practice, we must work with each one of these dimensions separately and then also integrate them. By that means, we can draw on all three dimensions at once.

We can never reach the point attained by the Japanese warriors if we follow the same path and the same method of training they did. To arrive at the summit of development, we must follow the shortest path, because our society does not allow for any detours. For that, we need a good guide, that is to say, a theory of progress on the path. My first aim in this book has been to analyze the structure of karate-do. Any method of making progress on the path must now be based on knowledge of this structure.

The method used to bring about development in karate nowadays is often an adaptation of that of other sports, whose structure is different. And this often leads to dead ends.

The notion of expanded time was an insight that allowed me to gain a deeper understanding of karate-do. It seems to me that when we experience expanded time, our unconscious mind manifests on the same level as our conscious mind. Not only during the practice of combat but also while exercising in katas and in the basic techniques, we should have as our aim to experience expanded time. This orientation is indispensable for achieving progress in karate goshin-do and getting beyond a certain plateau.

I have noticed that when my Western students concentrate, most of the time their form of concentration does not live up to my expectations. The notion of expanded time helped me to understand why. The Western style of concentration can be described as a bundle of awareness that is focused very strongly on, and therefore limited to, a very definite field. Concentration in Japanese culture is a sort of explosion, a sudden expansion, an opening out to a maximal area of awareness. In the course of this expansion, the boundary between the unconscious and the conscious mind is displaced. Verbalization is relegated to a secondary level.

For Westerners, acquiring this form of concentration should happen in the context of making a relationship between the two cultures on the most profound level.

NOTES

INTRODUCTION

1. Feudal society lasted in Japan until the Meiji Restoration in 1868.
2. Yagyu Munenori, *Heiho Kaden Sho*. A seventeenth-century book connected with the author's particular family tradition of the practice of the sword.
3. In the course of the process of modernization in Japan since the end of the nineteenth century, the value of many works of art and precious ancient documents has depreciated, and a significant number of them have been destroyed.

CHAPTER 1: WHAT IS KARATE?

1. This was Lord Shimazu, who ruled the region of Satsuma in the far south of Japan.
2. Written by a Taoist master named Hui Hai.
3. This also includes the transformation of the names of certain

katas that were Japanified at the time karate was being established in Japan. Owing to this historical development, it is currently possible for there to be a single kata that, in different styles, can have a Chinese, an Okinawan, or a Japanese name.

4. See Taisen Deshimaru, *The Zen Way to Martial Arts* (New York: Penguin, 1992).

5. The same idea is found when we analyze the ideogram for *bu*. The character *bu*, meaning "martial art or weapon," is composed of the two characters meaning "to stop" and "spear." This suggests the ability to stop the spear of the opponent and at the same time to stop our own spear, with "spear" symbolizing the whole of the force of an attack.

CHAPTER 2: BUDO AND KARATE GOSHIN-DO

1. The moving force behind the revolution that put an end to the feudal period was the hierarchically lowest rank of the warrior class. And it was mainly this group that played the leading role at the beginning of the modern period.

2. Chie Nakane, *Japanese Society* (Berkeley and Los Angeles: University of California Press, 1972).

3. Tsugumasa Nango, *Budo No Riron* (The Theory of Budo; Tokyo: Sanichi-Shobo Publications, 1972). Not translated.

4. An analytic attempt to determine the structure of goshin-do will enable us to gain a better understanding of do. But, I repeat, the notion of do will be analyzed here from the viewpoint of practice as opposed to anything sociological. What I mean by the sociological approach would be to analyze it in terms of the intersubjectivity of human relations or in connection with the multiple hierarchies of the social classes.

5. In the case of a form of budo using a weapon, such as kendo (Japanese fencing), this shell is not so hard and not so thick, because it is possible to enter more directly into the realm of

a many-sided technical learning process from the moment one has a sword in one's hand, whereas in bare-handed budo, one has to create the equivalent of weapons using one's body alone. Thus, one has to learn the technical forms for weapon-like deployment of the parts of the body before beginning to work on the other aspects.

CHAPTER 4: THE DIMENSIONS OF MAAI AND HYOSHI

1. Authors of this period use the words *ma* and *maai* interchangeably.
2. For example, the range of a punch with arm extended is often longer for a taller combatant, but the shorter combatant can start a kick at a distance that is too short to permit the taller one to reply in kind. All the punching and kicking techniques can be executed at a variety of distances. Therefore adopting a certain distance depends on determining the relationship of a number of complex factors.
3. It is clear that mere aging has nothing to do with progress in these other two dimensions. Progress can only be brought about by means of continuous training directed in a concrete way toward further development. Up until the beginning of the twentieth century, there continued to be living adepts of the disciplines that arose during the feudal period or adepts who had been their students and been trained directly by them. These adepts were able to offer their disciples an experiential perspective for making progress on the path, a perspective that was based on a cultural image derived directly from tradition. These adepts are the contemporary older masters I have been talking about. But in the course of the social evolution Japanese society has been undergoing and continues to undergo up to the present, ongoing changes in lifestyle have resulted in an ever-decreasing number of these

traditional adherents of the Way. This decrease has been going on since the end of the nineteenth century. That is why at the present time, very few of these masters are left. In order to make practical progress in the martial arts, we must now have a theory of budo. There are two main reasons for this. First of all, an institutionalization of the tradition is taking place, and it is extremely difficult to come in direct contact with these old masters in a way that would enable us to enter into the experiential perspective they offer. Second, almost no one in contemporary society is capable of following the lifestyle of these old masters, who even before the War were living on the fringes of the society of their time.

4. *Bushido: The Soul of Japan* (New York: G. P. Putnam's Sons, 1905) was written first in English in order to introduce Japanese "moral values" to the countries of the West.

5. Zeami (1363–1443) is considered the greatest director of Noh theater. He wrote not only Noh plays but also essays on Noh that exercised great influence on various areas of Japanese culture. *Shi Ka Do* can be translated "the way that leads to the state of a flower."

6. This book is one of the parts of the *Heiho Kaden Sho* (see introduction, note 2).

7. This means halting attacks executed with kime at a distance of zero to three centimeters (1.2 inches) from the face or vital points and cleanly halting blows to the belly or the most solid parts of the body at the point of touching the skin.

CHAPTER 5: THE DIMENSION OF YOMI

1. This period is also called the Edo period.

2. This group was charged with indispensable tasks that were forbidden by religion to the general population, such as cleaning execution sites, cleaning and burying the bodies of the executed, disposing of garbage, and so on.

3. *Budo Sho Shin Shu* "Fundamental Thought of the Way of

the Warrior," by Daidoji Yuzan (c. 1700). The influence of this book lasted in Japan until the end of the Second World War.

4. That is to say, a formalization of their way of being that corresponded to a restrictive social demand. See pp. 82–86 for the notion of "kata."

5. In the Japan of this period, people slept on their backs with their heads resting on a rather rigid pillow. The image of getting up is first of all that of raising one's head. The phrase "grabbing the pillow" thus expresses the idea of not even allowing the person to raise his head.

6. In the manner of an arrow.

7. See p. 179

8. *Fudochi Shimmyo Roku* (Immovable Wisdom). This work by Takuan is addressed to Yagyu Munenori, and became a major influence on warriors. It deals with the state of mind that must be acquired in order to practice the art of the sword.

9. See the work on this subject cited in chapter 2—*Japanese Society*, by Chie Nakane.

CHAPTER 6: FIVE SWORD MASTERS OF THE TOKUGAWA PERIOD

1. In the Japanese empire, the shogun held the real power. The emperor's power was primarily symbolic.

2. I give a literal translation of this paragraph in order not to distort its meaning. The word *nen*, which I translate here as "thought," has a very broad meaning in Japanese; it refers to any conscious mental state or function: ideas, feelings, desires, and so on. There is no word in English that covers the same range of meaning.

3. See chapter 4.

4. D. T. Suzuki, *Zen Buddhism: Selected Writings of D. T. Suzuki*, edited by William Barrett (New York: Three Rivers Press, 1996), 350–52.

5. A weapon halfway between a sword and a spear. The blade and the handle are both quite long.

6. The name of this hyoshi can have two meanings in Japanese. It is usually understood to mean "the second hyoshi of the hip." Personally, I understand it in the sense of "hyoshi carried out in two phases."

7. A kind of mythical monkey with very short arms.

8. Tengu is a god with a red head and a very long nose, often represented in Japanese sculpture. He is considered to be the specialist among the gods in the martial arts.

9. *Zan* means "to subsist" or "to remain." *Shin* means "the mind."

GLOSSARY

aikido: Art of bare-handed combat that seeks to overcome the opponent without blows. It was founded in the twentieth century by Master Ueshiba.

ainuke: Combat situation in which neither combatant wins or loses. Ainuke tends in the direction of transcending combat.

bo: A stick.

bokken: A wooden sword traditionally used for training.

budo: Literally, "way of the martial arts." This term refers to all of the traditional Japanese martial arts.

bushi: Traditional name for the Japanese warrior. Synonym of samurai.

chudan: Middle part of the body (belly).

deai: Particular form of counter-maneuver.

do: Literally, "way," or "path"; from the Chinese *tao*.

dojo: Literally, "place where the way is found." The name given to training halls.

Ekkinkyo: The method of physical training taught by Bodhidharma. It was based on an affirmation of the unity of body and mind.

gedan: Lower part of the body.

goshin-do: The way of the human defense (or self-defense).

hara gei: Literally, the art or technique of the belly (*hara*), or gut. This refers to people being able to know each other's minds intuitively, without thoughts being explicitly expressed.

hyoshi: Integration of cadences that rhythmically bind one or several persons and their environment within the framework of a planned cultural activity. This results in balance or overall harmony.

jodan: Upper part of the body.

jutsu: Technique or method.

kado: Literally, "the way of flowers"; the art of flower arranging.

kamikaze: Literally, "the wind of the gods." This refers to pilots who, during the Second World War, departed for battle in their planes without any hope of survival.

karate: Literally, "bare-handed." An art of bare-handed combat in which one confronts the adversary from a distance. The principal techniques are punches and kicks to vital points, complemented by holds and throws when the adversary is close.

karate-do: The way of karate.

kata: Literally, "form," or "mold." A sequence composed of formalized and codified movements supported by a sense of seeking the way. In karate, the katas have a mnemono-technical function.

kendo: Literally, "the way of the sword." An art of combat developed by the Japanese warriors of feudal times.

kiai: This term has two senses: (1) a shout; and (2) connecting with (grasping in the belly) ki, the energy that fills the universe and that is the essence of everything.

kyudo: The way of archery.

maai: Literally, *ma* means "distance" or "interval"; *ai* means "to meet" (with a movement). This term expresses the idea of an interval or distance and at the same time that of moving closer or farther away.

Meiji period: Period from 1868 to 1912, corresponding to the reign of the emperor Meiji.

muto: Literally, "without a sword." A technique for fighting without a weapon against an adversary armed with a sword.

naginata: A weapon halfway between a sword and a spear; both the handle and the blade are quite long.

Noh: A very ancient form of Japanese theater.

nunchaku: A weapon composed of two joined sticks. It is derived from the farmer's flail.

okinawa-te: Literally, "Okinawa hand." This term refers to combat techniques traditionally thought to be developed on the island of Okinawa. Karate originated from these techniques.

sado: The way of tea.

sakki: The atmosphere created by the intent to kill.

samurai: Synonym of *bushi*.

shaolin-su kempo: A combat technique that originated from the teaching of Bodhidharma and was developed at Shaolin-su (Shorin-ji) Temple in China.

shogun: High feudal dignitary, who under the reign of the Japanese emperors of the feudal period, often held the effective political power.

shotokan: Name of the karate dojo of Gichin Funakoshi. It remains the principal dojo of his style of karate.

tai: This term has two meanings: (1) "to wait" and is opposed to *ken,* meaning "to attack"; and (2) "body," an object that is opposed to yu.

to-de: Literally, "Chinese hand," a name that is also given in Japan to okinawa-te.

Tokugawa period: Period dominated by the family of the Tokugawa shoguns (1603–1868).

tonfa: A short piece of wood with a perpendicularly mounted handle.

yomi: The art of intuitively sensing and foreseeing.

yu: The essential function of things.

Zen: True and profound silence. A form of Buddhism developed in China (Ch'an in Chinese), then in Japan, in which sitting meditation without a meditation object (zazen) is practiced.

NAMES AND WORKS CITED

CHUANG TZU (fourth century B.C.E.)

A Chinese Taoist philosopher, called Son Shi in Japanese.

BODHIDHARMA (fourth century C.E.)

A Buddhist monk of Indian origin who traveled to China, where he taught the fundamentals of Zen Buddhism. He also expounded a method of physical training, Ekkinkyo, which is one of the sources of the Chinese bare-handed combat techniques.

ZEAMI (1363-1443)

A celebrated author and actor of the Noh theater who wrote *Shi Ka Do* (The Way that Leads to the State of a Flower).

YAGYU MUNENORI (1571-1646)

A sword master and author of *Heiho Kaden Sho* (The Life-Giving Sword), a book on his family tradition of swordsmanship; and *Gyoku Sei Shu*, a treatise on weapons.

TAKUAN (1573-1645)

A Buddhist monk, he wrote *Fudochi Shimmyo Roku* (The Unfettered Mind).

MIYAMOTO MUSASHI (1584-1646)

A master of the sword who wrote *Go Rin No Sho* (Writings on the Five Wheels), commonly known as *The Book of Five Rings*.

ITO ITTOSAI (end of the sixteenth and beginning of the seventeenth centuries)

A master of the sword who emphasized the importance of maai in combat.

KOTODA YAHEI (seventeenth century)

Author of *Ittosai Sensei Kempo Sho* (Writings on the Sword Master Ito Ittosai).

ISSAI CHOZANSHI (pseudonym of Niwa Jurozaemon; 1619-1741)

A master of the sword, he was also the author of numerous works, one of which is *Tengu Gei Jutsu Ron* (Questions to a God on the Art of the Sword).

DAIDOJI YUZAN (late seventeenth to early eighteenth century)

A samurai who wrote the *Budo Sho Shin Shu*, which presents the basic philosophy of the way of the warrior.

MATSUURA SEIZAN (b. 1760)

A master of the sword and man of letters, he was the author of numerous works, including *Joseishi Kendan* (Words on Swordsmanship).

KENKICHI SAKAKIBARA (1830-1894)

A sword master of the Tokugawa period.

YAMAOKA TESSHU (1836-1888)

One of the greatest sword masters of the Meiji period and a devoted practitioner of Zen.

GICHIN FUNAKOSHI (1868-1917)

A master of okinawa-te who introduced the term *karate-do*. He wrote *Karate Nijika Jo* (Twenty Precepts of Karate-do) and *Karate Do Kyohan* (Texts on Karate-do).

D. T. SUZUKI (1870–1966)

A Buddhist scholar and seminal figure in the transmission of Zen philosophy to the West. He taught widely throughout Japan, the United States, and Europe, and was the author of numerous books and essays on Buddhism and Zen.

MORIHEI UESHIBA (1883–1969)

The founder of Aikido, a contemporary budo art.

INAZO NITOBE (late nineteenth century)

A professor and author of *Bushido: The Soul of Japan*, which he wrote in English.

TAISEN DESHIMARU (1914–1982)

A Buddhist monk of Japanese origin who came to Europe at the end of 1967 and spread the teachings of Zen Buddhism there.

CHIE NAKANE (b. 1926)

A contemporary anthropologist, and the author of *Tate Shakei No Ningen Kankei*, which was translated and published in an American paperback edition by the University of California Press as *Japanese Society* (Berkeley and Los Angeles, 1972).

TSUGUMASA NANGO (contemporary)

Karate master who wrote *Budo No Riron* (The Theory of Budo).

BOOKS BY KENJI TOKITSU AVAILABLE FROM SHAMBHALA PUBLICATIONS

The Complete Book of Five Rings

Modern martial arts master Kenji Tokitsu illuminates Miyamoto Musashi's classic, *The Book of Five Rings*, in this authoritative translation. *The Complete Book of Five Rings* includes extensive notes and commentary, as well as translations of four lesser-known works by Musashi: "*The Mirror of the Way of Strategy*," which Musashi wrote when he was in his twenties; "*Thirty-five Instructions on Strategy*," and "*Forty-two Instructions on Strategy*," which were precursors to *The Book of Five Rings*; and "*The Way to Be Followed Alone*," which Musashi wrote just days before his death. Read together, these five texts provide a detailed and nuanced view of Musashi's ideas on swordsmanship, strategy, and self-cultivation.

Ki and the Way of the Martial Arts

While technical prowess and physical power are essential characteristics of a martial artist, true mastery of the art comes by cultivating one's inner strength. Here, Kenji Tokitsu shows how cultivating *ki* (life force) and understanding the principles of budo (the martial path of self-development) can make training in martial arts more meaningful, effective, and personally and spiritually rewarding. Tokitsu emphasizes the mental aspects of martial arts practice, such as the importance of ki development, *seme* (capturing your opponent's mind), and understanding *ma* (the spatial relationship in combat). He also gives a historical and cultural survey of budo, and explains how the Western view of budo training is different than the Japanese—a perspective rarely available to Western martial artists.

Miyamoto Musashi: His Life and Writings

Miyamoto Musashi, who lived in Japan in the fifteenth century, was a renowned samurai warrior. He has become a martial arts icon, known not just as an undefeated dueler, but also as a master of battlefield strategy. In this vivid and meticulously researched biography, Kenji Tokitsu turns a critical eye on Musashi's life and writings, separating fact from fiction, and providing a view of the man and his ideas that is accessible and relevant to today's readers and martial arts students. This book includes Tokitsu's translation of several works by Musashi, including *The Book of Five Rings* in its entirety, as well as color-reproductions of Musashi's calligraphies and paintings, with commentary by the well-known art historian Stephen Addiss.